*Lives of*

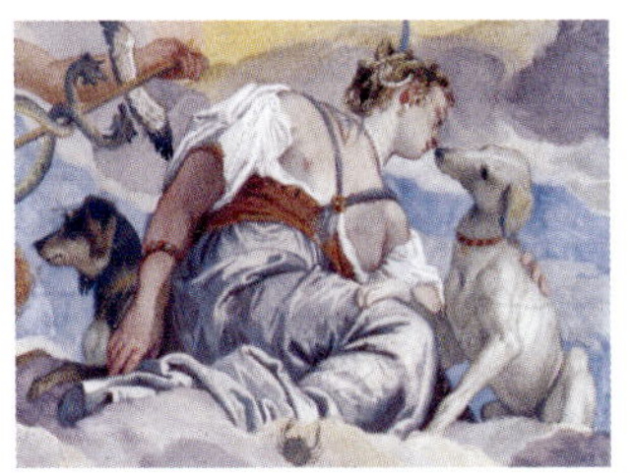

*Paolo Veronese*

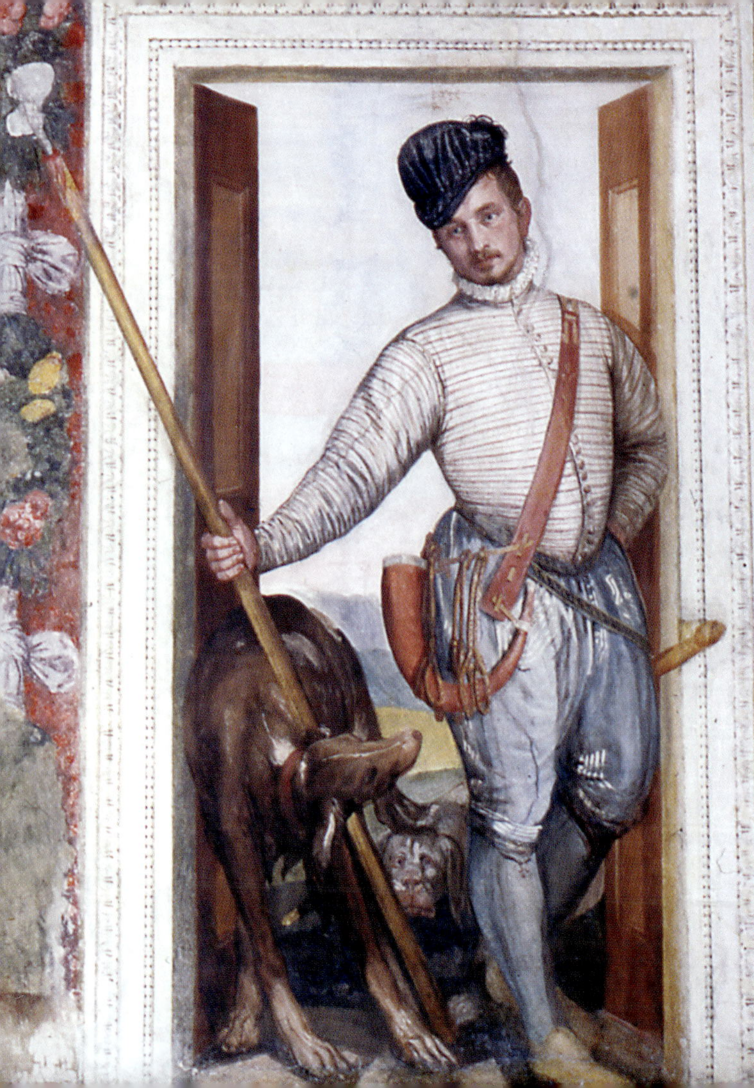

# LIVES OF
# VERONESE

BY

GIORGIO VASARI,

RAFFAELE BORGHINI,

AND

CARLO RIDOLFI

*Translated and with an introduction by*

XAVIER F. SALOMON

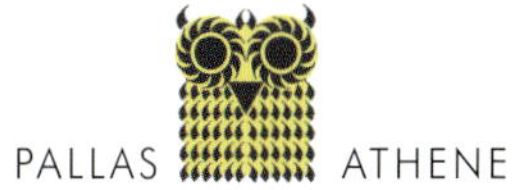

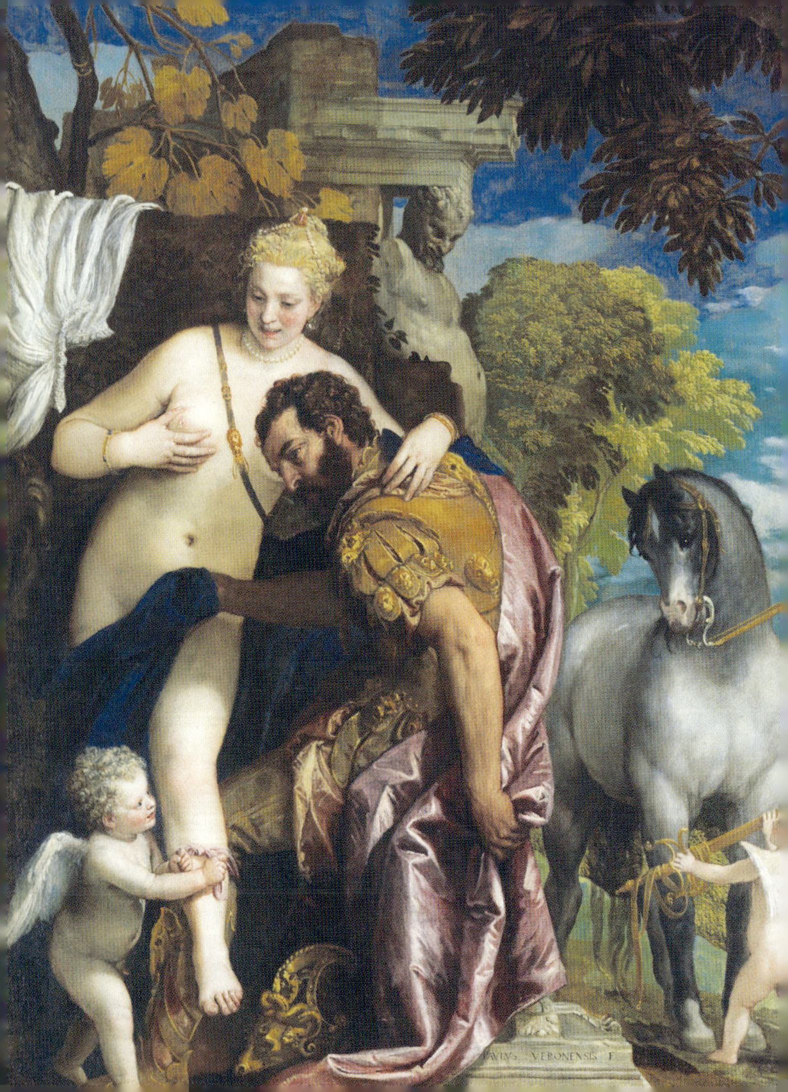
PAVLVS VERONENSIS F

# CONTENTS



*Opposite: Mars and Venus united by Love, c. 1570-75*

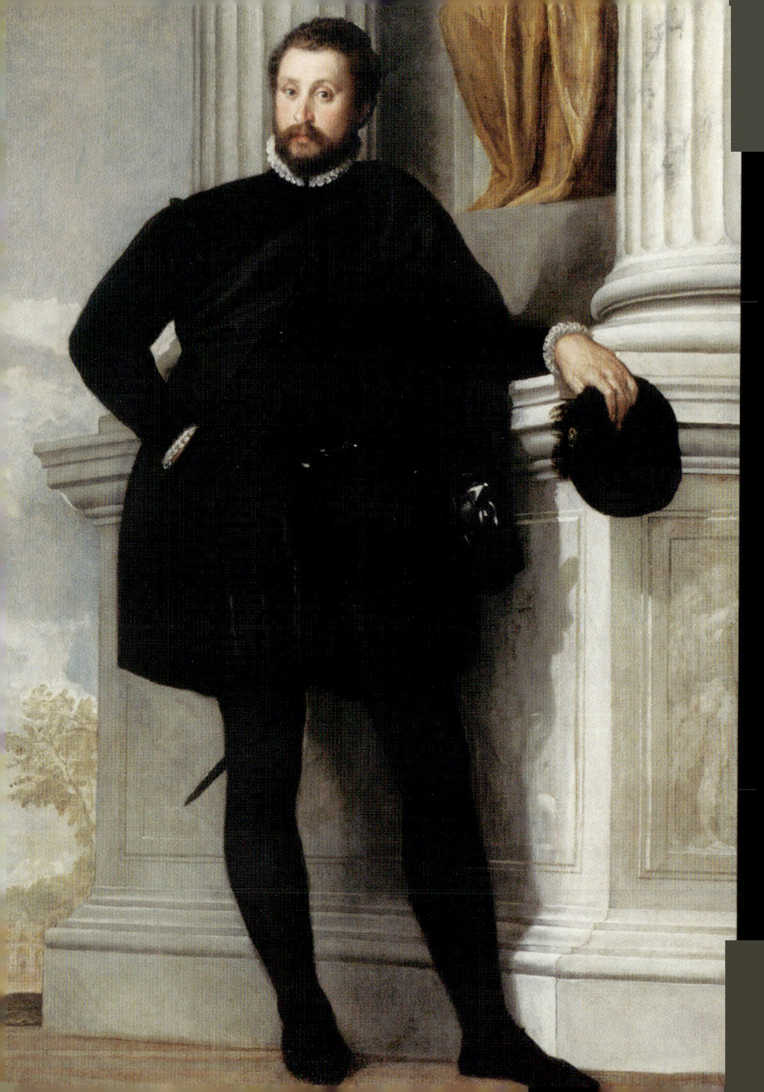

# INTRODUCTION

*XAVIER F. SALOMON*

*On 11 March 1553, four young painters from Verona presented a petition to Cardinal Ercole Gonzaga in Mantua. A year earlier, Battista del Moro (1514-74), Domenico Brusasorci (1516-67), Paolo Farinati (1524-1606) and Paolo Veronese (1528-88), had been commissioned to paint four altarpieces for chapels in the cathedral of Mantua. The paintings were now ready and the artists complained that not only had they not been paid, but no one had even come to collect the paintings. A prestigious public commission from a cardinal for the foreign Gonzaga court in Mantua was a sign of great favour for the four painters, and especially for Paolo, who at twenty-four was the youngest of the quartet. Veronese signed the document as Paolo Spezapreda, as a reference to his training as a stonecutter. Both his father, Gabriele (b. 1497), and grandfather, Piero (b. 1474) were* spezaprede, *and Paolo's elder brother Francesco (b. 1520) had also followed in the family's footsteps.*

*Opposite: Portrait of a man, ca. 1565. At one stage thought to be a self-portrait*

*Only three years before the petition to Cardinal Gonzaga, Giorgio Vasari (1511-74) had published in Florence his influential* Lives of the Painters, Sculptors, and Architects, *in which he compiled the biographies of the foremost artists of the past and of his own age, culminating in the* Life *of Michelangelo. For the most part, the artists in Vasari's* Lives *were Tuscan. The third book, dedicated to the artists of what Vasari called the 'maniera moderna', included a few Venetians: Giorgione, Girolamo da Treviso, Palma il Vecchio, Lorenzo Lotto, and Sebastiano del Piombo. Considering Vasari's interests and the scope of the work, it is hardly surprising that in the 1550 edition of the* Lives, *there was no mention of the young stonecutter Paolo from Verona.*

*Paolo, however, had already decided to abandon his family's career and, aged thirteen, in 1541, he was recorded as training and living in the house of the painter Antonio Badile in Verona. In 1551, Paolo was at work on his first significant commission, when, together with Battista Zelotti, he decorated the Villa Soranza at Treville. A year later came the Gonzaga commission for the altarpiece in Mantua. The documentation linked to the Mantua project is also the last mention of Paolo in Verona; by 1555 he was established in Venice, renting a studio in the parish of Santi Apostoli. With his move to Venice, Veronese's career took off. Paolo's artistic skills were already manifest in his early works and patrons admired his style, so eloquently described by Marco Boschini in 1660: 'the supreme Gods allowed him [Veronese] to insert their portraits in his works; and because of this every figure by Paolo has something celestial. Architecture put into his hands the most well-conceived and proportioned outlines, which I wish someone would use in the most decorous buildings. Invention has made him its arbiter in placing and ordering groups in narratives, decorating them with the most weighty forms and expressions of characters, so sumptuously dressed, that they might serve as model and instructions for princes and how they should appear majestic in front of the world. In conclusion, all the Graces had the ambition of always assisting him; so that he can be called the delight of the world, because in him there is everything that one would look for in pictorial art and in universal taste'. Already in 1553, he had been working on part of the ceiling for the Hall of the Council of Ten in the Doge's Palace – the political and social heart of the city – and under such good early auspices, the career that followed was remarkable. In 1555 came the commissions for paintings at San Sebastiano and the altarpiece for the high altar of the cathedral of Montagnana. In the contract for the Montagnana* Transfiguration, *of 3 June 1555, Paolo had already abandoned Spezapreda as his surname and had taken the more*

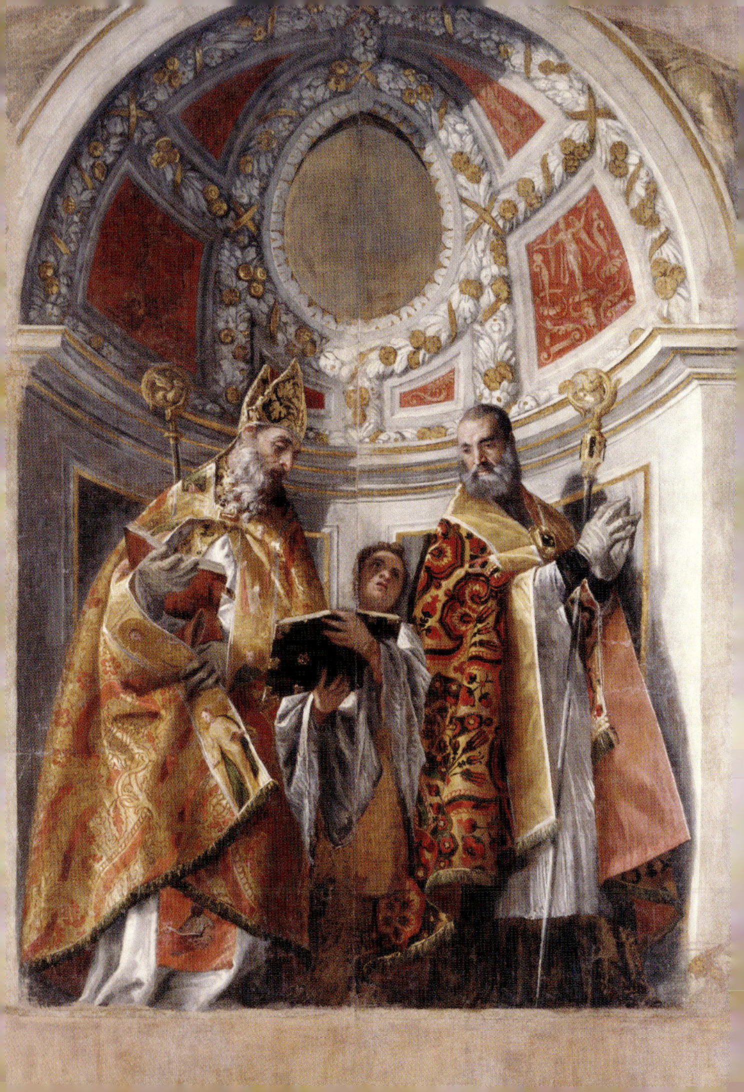

*glamorous and aristocratic name of Caliari, which he was to use for the rest of his life.*

*By the time Vasari reviewed his* Lives *and published a second version of them 'almost completely done anew' in 1568, other contemporary artists from the Veneto had been added to the third book: Fra Giocondo, Liberale da Verona, Matteo dal Nassaro, Battista Franco, and Titian. Paolo Veronese, forty years old and remarkably successful, was included, but no full life was dedicated to him. Between the lives of Girolamo and Bartolomeo Genga, and that of Sodoma, Vasari included the biography of his good friend, the Veronese architect Michele Sanmicheli. Within this* Life, *Vasari incorporated that of Sanmicheli's nephew Gian Girolamo, and a series of short biographies of young painters from Verona 'worthy of being mentioned' ('altri valenthuomini veronesi'). These were Domenico del Riccio (Brusasorci) and his son Felice, Bernardino India, Eliodoro Forbicini, Battista Zelotti and Paolo Veronese – whom Sanmicheli 'loved as if they were his own sons' – and Paolo Farinati. The few pages Vasari dedicated to Veronese can be considered as a 'life' to all intents and purposes, as they represent the first contemporary account which includes essential information*

*Opposite: Saints Geminianus and Severus, ca. 1560*

*on his early career. Paolo also made a few intermittent appearances in the lives of other artists. In the short biography of Domenico Brusasorci, Vasari recorded the Mantua commission in full: 'what moved the Duke to commission that altarpiece [for Santa Barbara in Mantua] was his having seen and much liked his manner in an altarpiece, which Domenico had painted long before in the cathedral of Mantua in the chapel of Saint Margaret, in competition with Paolino, who executed that of Saint Anthony, with Paolo Farinati, who painted that of Saint Martin, and with Battista del Moro, who executed that of the Magdalene. All which four artists from Verona had been summoned there by Cardinal Ercole of Mantua, in order to adorn that church, which had been reconstructed by him following the design of Giulio Romano.' The same commission was reported in the lives of Paolo Farinati and in that of Garofalo and Girolamo da Carpi. Veronese's painting was there described in full: 'and one, which was the best of the group, although all of them are most beautiful, in which is Saint Anthony Abbot beaten by the devil in the guise of a woman, who tempts him, is by the hand of Paolo Veronese'. In the same biography, writing about Mantua*

*Opposite: The Temptation of St Anthony, 1552*

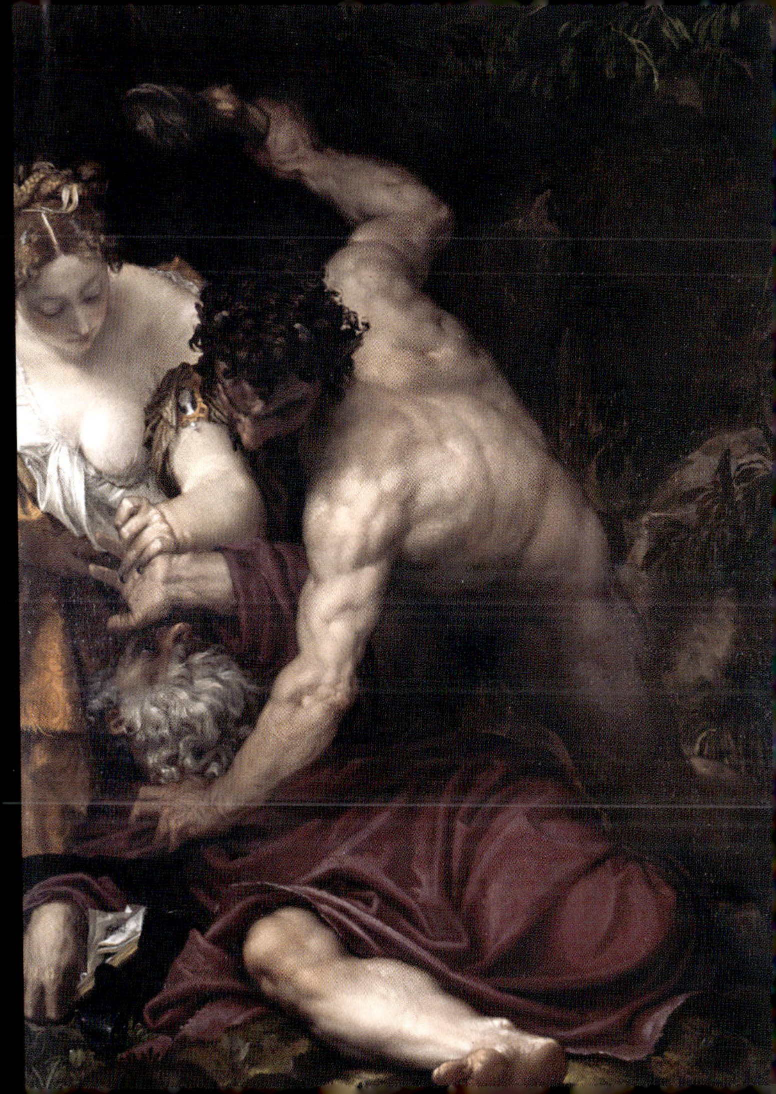

*and its surroundings, Vasari also mentioned the altarpieces in the abbey church of San Benedetto Po and especially 'three by Paolo Veronese, which are the best'. In the life of Battista Zelotti, instead, Vasari listed some of Veronese's earliest works painted together with Battista: the frescoes for the Da Porto family in Thiene, the Villa Soranza, the façade of the house of Antonio Cappello in Venice, and the ceiling for the Hall of the Council of Ten.*

*Vasari's biography of Paolo – endearingly called 'Paolino' because of his young age (Vasari records him as being just over thirty, while in fact Paolo was forty by the time the* Lives *were published) – demonstrates the high esteem in which Veronese was already held. An early period of study under Giovanni Caroto is not mentioned by other sources, but otherwise Vasari accurately proceeded to record Veronese's early works, from the Da Porto and Soranza to Villa Barbaro at Maser, from the great Venetian public commissions (the Doge's Palace and San Sebastiano) to the magnificent* Feasts *painted for refectories (those for San Nazaro in Verona, and the* Marriage Feast at Cana *for San Giorgio Maggiore where 'if I remember well, one can see there more than a hundred and fifty heads, all different and painted with great care'). Already by the mid-1560s some of Veronese's works were disappearing and Vasari recorded the fact: the frescoed façade of the house of a merchant which 'the sea-air is*

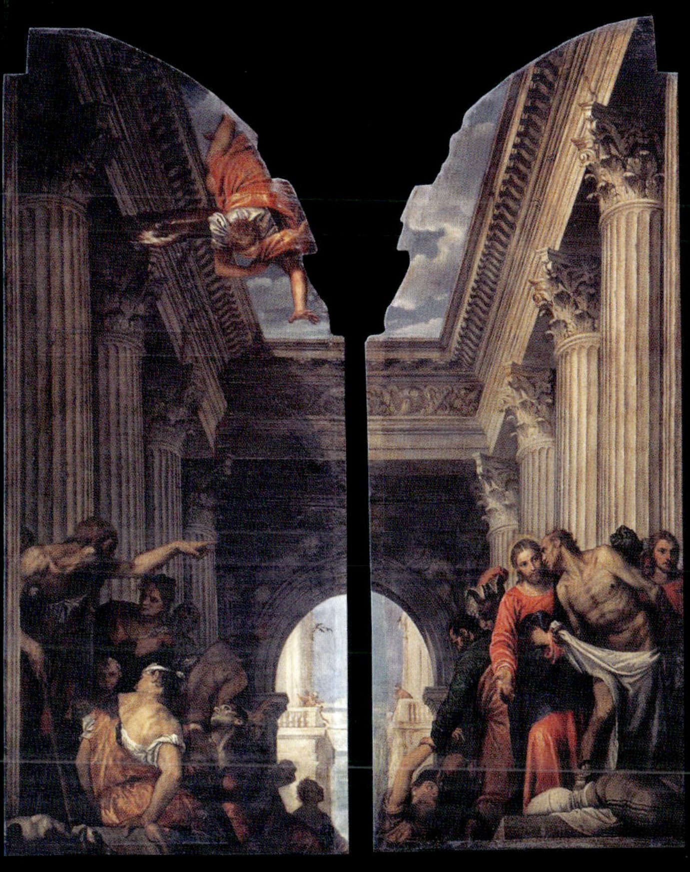

*Christ at the Pool of Bethesda, ca. 1560*
*–organ shutters at San Sebastiano*

*consuming slowly'. Vasari seemed to have been particularly keen on the idea of competitions between artists, not only in the case of the Mantuan canvases, but also in the passing references in the life of Tintoretto (included in the life of Battista Franco) of Veronese's participation in the competitions for the Hall of the Great Council and for the Scuola di San Rocco. Vasari, indeed, concluded Veronese's life with a detailed account of the competition for the ceiling of the Library of Saint Mark's in 1556-57, and of Paolo's victory over his colleagues.*

*Vasari's account of Veronese's first twenty years of activity is remarkably accurate, if short. Considering the writer's renowned bias for everything Florentine it is significant that a few pages were dedicated to Paolo at all. About thirty years later, however, the painter Annibale Carracci did not agree. In his annotations to Vasari's* Lives *he indignantly commented: 'I have known this Paolino and I have seen his beautiful works. He deserves to have a great volume written in praise of him, for his pictures prove that he is second to no other painter, and this fool passes over him in four lines. And just because he was not Florentine.'*

*Veronese's next biographer, Raffaele Borghini (1537-1588) was also Florentine. In 1584, almost twenty years after Vasari's* Lives, *he published* Il Riposo di Raffaele Borghini in cui della pittura e della scultura si favella, de' più famose opere loro si fa menzione, e le cose principali appartenenti a dette arti s'ingegnano *('The "Riposo" of Raffaele Borghini, in which painting and sculpture are discussed, the most famous works are mentioned, and the main elements of those arts are taught'). Not strictly biographical,* Il Riposo *is a compendium of artistic theory and lists of works by famous artists. Inevitably Borghini relied profoundly on Vasari. The text, divided in four books, takes the form of imaginary dialogues which take place between Bernardo Vecchietti, Baccio Valori, Girolamo Michelozzi and Ridolfo Sirigatti, in Vecchietti's villa of 'Il Riposo' outside Florence. When Borghini's book was published, Veronese was still alive, at the end of his career. Borghini provided in his short biography of Veronese more information than Vasari. He correctly reported that Paolo had studied with Antonio Badile (rather than Giovanni Caroto), but mistakenly thought that Badile was Veronese's uncle. In terms of Paolo's early career, Borghini wrote about most of the public works already mentioned by Vasari (the Mantua altarpiece, the ceiling of the Hall of the Council of Ten, the tondi for the Library, the altarpieces for San Benedetto Po) but focused mainly on Veronese's* Feasts *for*

*Overleaf: Christ among the Doctors, ca. 1560*

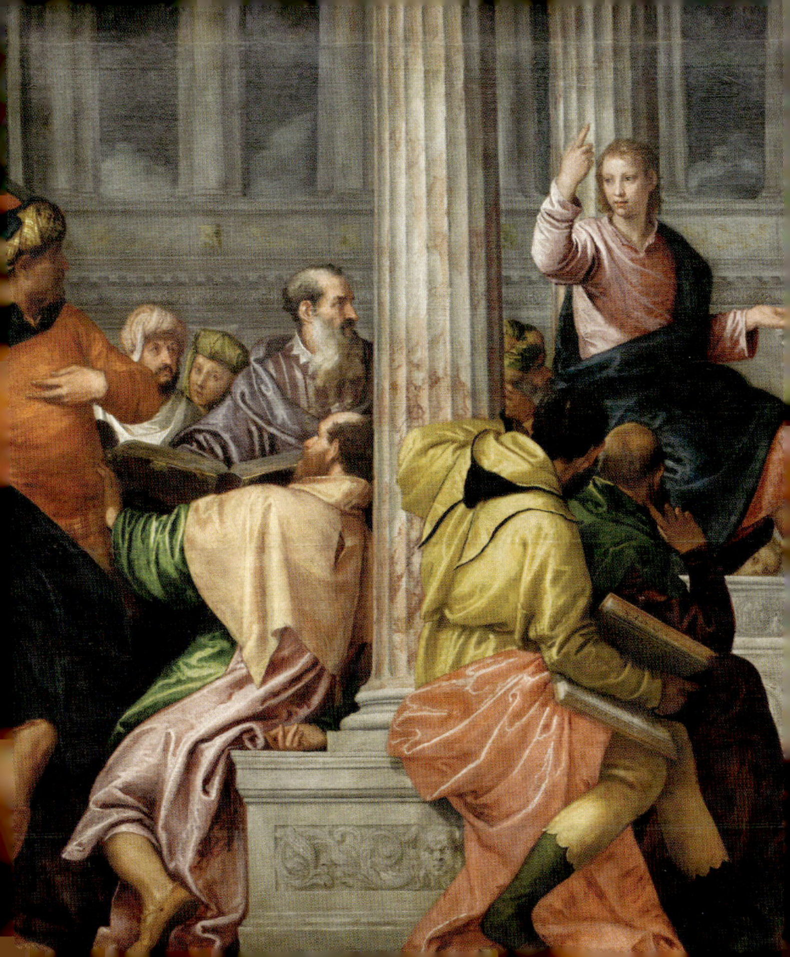

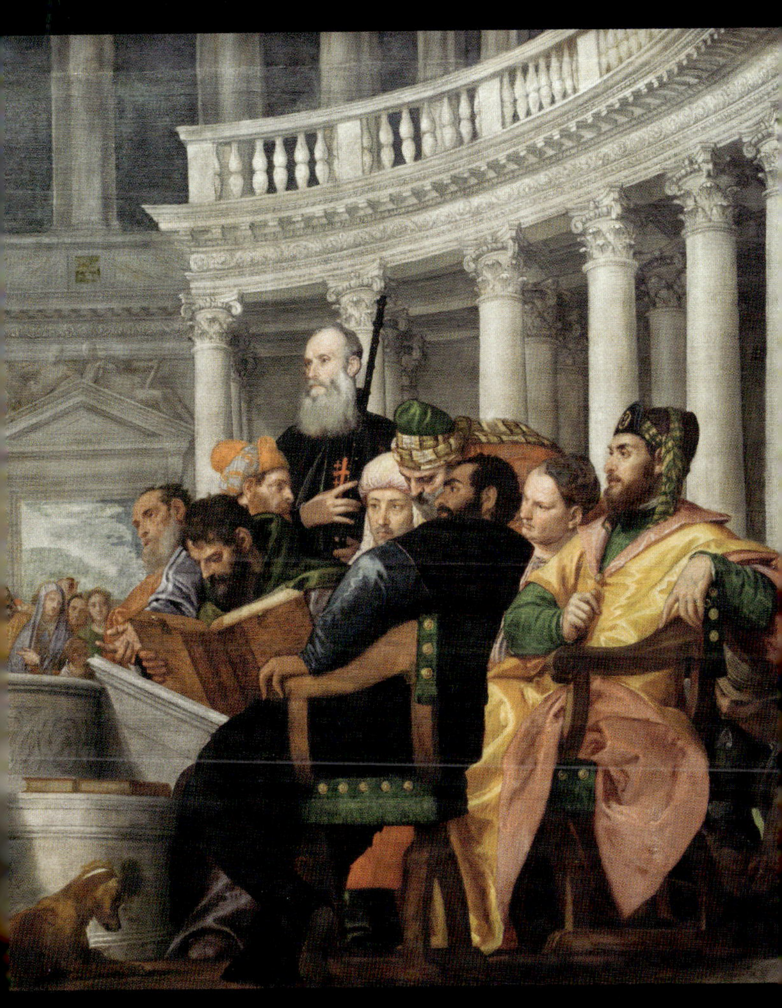

*various refectories. The list of Venetian works included many of his altarpieces (the Pala Bonaldi, the* Mystic Marriage of Saint Catherine, *the high altar of San Sebastiano, and the three for San Francesco della Vigna). Often, unfortunately, Borghini seemed to confuse titles of works and places (Vasari was more precise): the altarpiece for Cardinal Gonzaga was destined for the cathedral of Mantua, and not for the church of Sant'Andrea; the high altar of San Giorgio in Braida in Verona is a* Martyrdom of Saint George, *not Saint Laurence; the* Feast in the House of Simon *was in the refectory of San Nazaro in Verona, not San Lorenzo (Borghini must have had a particular predilection for Saint Laurence!); and the painting for Monte Berico in Vicenza, was a* Feast of Saint Gregory the Great, *rather than a* Last Supper. *Apart from these inaccuracies, Borghini was well-informed. He mentioned paintings that Veronese had sent abroad, four for the Duke of Savoy, and a* Venus, Mars and Weeping Cupid *and a* Venus at the Mirror *for the emperor. The most recent works that Borghini described were the pendant* Venus and Adonis *and* Cephalus and Procris, *painted in the late 1570s. Like Vasari, Borghini thought that Veronese was younger than reality; he concluded the few pages on Paolo commenting that he was 'now fifty-two years old, and he has not ceased from painting continuously to great advantage'. Veronese was by then fifty-*

*six and died four years after Borghini's* Riposo *was published. After catching a pulmonary infection during a religious procession near his country house at Sant'Angelo, outside Treviso, he returned to Venice, where he died on 19 April 1588.*

*The artist's third – and most comprehensive biography – is probably also the most useful for its complete and accurate account of the painter's life and work. Carlo Ridolfi (1594-1658), a painter, collector of drawings, and writer, had published full biographies of Jacopo Tintoretto in 1642 and of Paolo Veronese in 1646. These texts were the foundation of a much wider project, possibly supported by the Venetian government, which resulted in the publication, in 1648, of* Le Maraviglie dell'Arte, ovvero le vite degli illustri pittori Veneti e dello stato, *a series of biographies of more than one hundred and fifty Venetian painters. Ridolfi responded with his book to Vasari and filled the gap in terms of Venetian art left by the* Lives. *Compared to Vasari and Borghini's short biographies of Veronese, Ridolfi's is the fullest and most detailed early account of the artist's career. Ridolfi had never met Veronese, but he had studied painting with Aliense, one of Paolo's pupils, and knew Giuseppe Caliari, Paolo's grandson. Ridolfi must have known Giuseppe well, as he was able fully to list the paintings that had remained in Paolo's house after his death (and that*

*Giuseppe still owned), and had even seen the famous gold chain that Titian and Sansovino had given to Veronese as a prize for the Library competition (also mentioned by Vasari and Borghini), which Giuseppe still kept as a 'precious relic of his glorious ancestor'.*

*Even though Ridolfi started by giving Veronese's wrong birth date (1530 instead of 1528) and followed Borghini's misguided claim that Badile was Paolo's uncle, he proceeded to accurately list and describe a large amount of paintings by Veronese, in Venice and abroad. It is thanks to Ridolfi's text that art historians have been able to identify the original patrons and location of many of Paolo's paintings. Ridolfi not only documented Veronese's public works, but also gave an extensive account of his pictures in private collections in the Veneto, and of paintings that have since been destroyed (for example the frescoes in Villa Soranza or the Pala Cuccina in San Francesco della Vigna). Understandably, Ridolfi's precision depended on the geographical location of the paintings. While in Venice and the Veneto his accuracy is usually impeccable, when it comes to foreign countries, the writer's information has to be taken with a pinch of salt. For example, Ridolfi listed three paintings made for Emperor Rudolph II:* Venus and

*Opposite: Judith and Holofernes, ca. 1585*

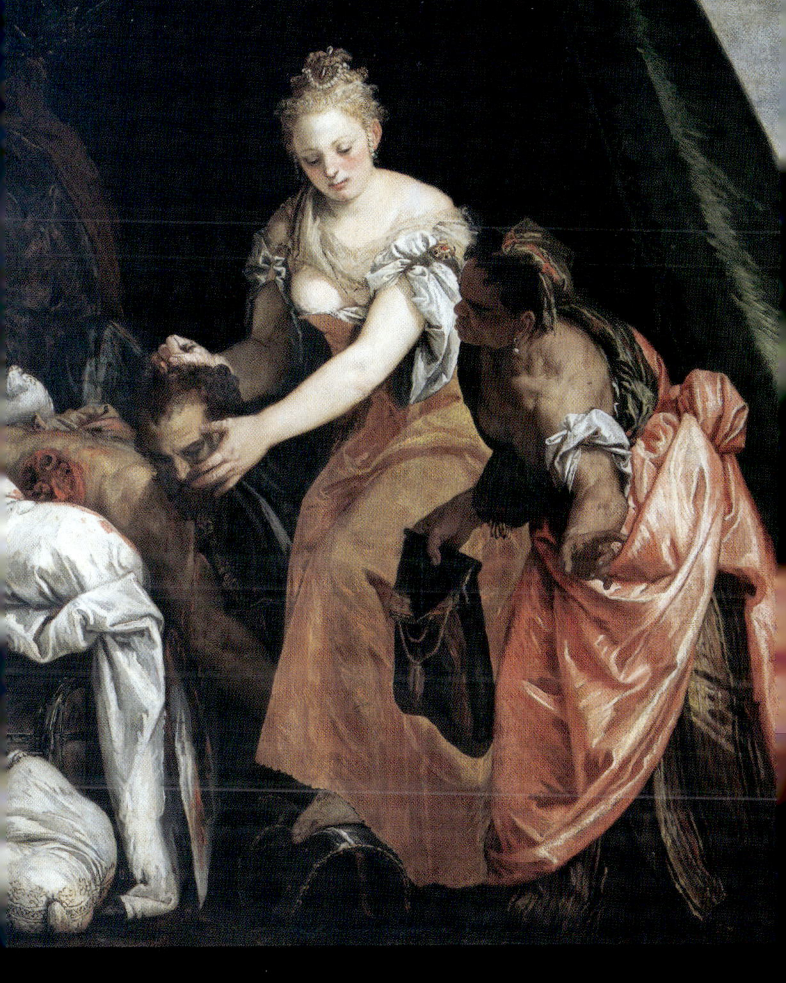

Mars, Venus at the Mirror, *and* Cephalus and Procris. *The information is probably directly lifted from Borghini, who had mentioned the first two works as made for the emperor (he probably meant Maximilian II), and had listed a* Cephalus and Procris *– as a pendant to* Venus and Adonis *– in the next sentence, without specifying its patron. Even when Ridolfi described paintings in contemporary collections he often failed to mention (and probably did not know) the works' original provenance. The two canvases by Veronese now in the Galleria Borghese in Rome, the* Saint John the Baptist preaching, *and the small* Saint Anthony of Padua preaching to the Fish, *are mentioned by Ridolfi as already being in Rome (both were in the Borghese collection by then, even if the first was mistakenly listed by him as being with Prince Ludovisi). It is unclear to this day who Veronese painted them for. The original location and patrons of significant paintings that are not mentioned by Ridolfi – for example the Petrobelli Altarpiece (now divided between the National Gallery of Canada, the Blanton Museum of Art, the Scottish National Gallery, and Dulwich Picture Gallery), or the* Rest on the Flight into Egypt *now at the Ringling Museum – have only been discovered relatively recently or still await to be identified.*

*Ridolfi, unlike Vasari and Borghini, also provided a vivid portrait of Veronese the man, no doubt supplied by his grandson. Paolo emerges as a gentle, self-effacing character, devout and virtuous. His art and his family (he had married his master Badile's daughter, Elena, in 1566) appear to have been his only concerns. His accomplishments and wealth only seem to be reflected in his fashion choices: 'he used precious clothes and velvet shoes'. We would like to know more about Veronese's private life, but, unfortunately, Vasari and Borghini's silence, and Ridolfi's scant information are all we have.*

*Ridolfi's biography is often interrupted by digressions which bring patronage and collecting in sixteenth-century Venice to life. The episode of the foolish nuns who had commissioned a* Paradise *by Veronese, but decided to substitute for it one by a cunning Flemish painter, who having got a 'gem' in exchange for his 'paste', promptly sold the painting by Paolo for 400 scudi, remains memorable. The biographer's prose is often florid and overflowing with rhetorical devices. Cecil Gould acerbically described Ridolfi's* Maraviglie *as 'rather for information than for pleasure'. But his comment that Ridolfi 'saw fit to adorn his rather arid history with festoons of classical allusions, and adulatory and high-flown verses addressed to his subjects' is clearly accurate. The prolix and grandiloquent sentences with which every work by Paolo is portrayed give way, at times, to rather poetic pages, such as the descriptions of the* Feast in the House of Simon *for San*

*Nazaro (of which Ridolfi had painted a copy for a Flemish collector), or the account of the paintings in San Sebastiano. Unforgettable is the description of the unattractive* Apparition of the Virgin to the Daughter of the King of France *(a workshop piece), in the collection of Girolamo Melchiori, the parish priest of Santa Fosca. The grisly saga of the royal princess, and her evil stepmother's failed attempts on her life, which resulted in the loss of her hands, miraculously returned to her by the Virgin, reads as a sixteenth-century version of Walt Disney's* Snow White, *tinted with all the horror and gory details of a tale by the Brothers Grimm.*

*Without Vasari, Borghini, and above all Ridolfi, art historians would be hard pressed today to delineate a coherent account of Veronese's career. It is surprising how much of what we know about the painter is still indebted to these three writers. A great volume on Veronese – as wished for by Annibale Carracci – was not published until much later. It was three hundred years after Veronese's death, in 1888, that Pietro Caliari, a direct descendant, wrote the first full monograph on the painter. Caliari's book with its transcribed documentation, remains to this day the basic text and starting point for any Veronese scholar, beyond these three early* Lives.

GIORGIO VASARI

# *Life of Paolo Caliari Veronese, Painter*

*from*

*Lives of the Most Eminent Painters, Sculptors and Architects*

1568

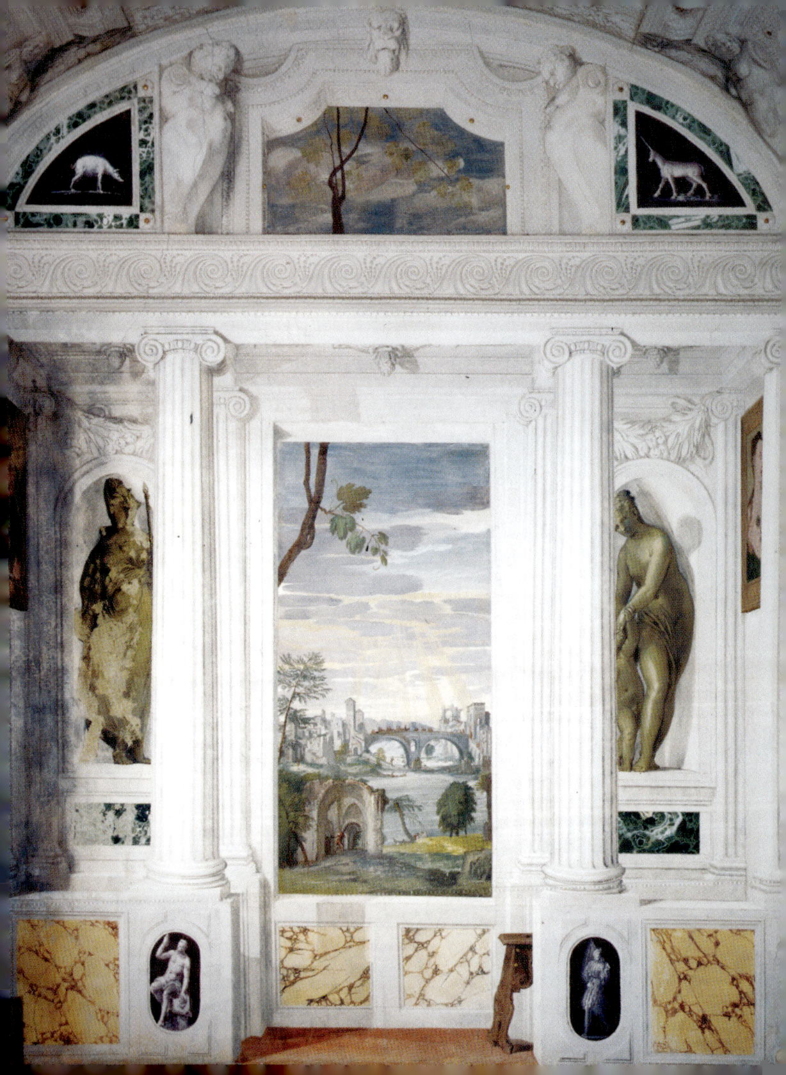

Also from Verona is a certain painter, Paolino, who is today held in very high esteem in Venice, because, not being more than thirty years old, he has painted many commendable things. Born in Verona from a *scarpellino*, or, as they say in that region, a *tagliapietre* (stonecutter), and having learnt the principles of painting from Giovanni Caroto from Verona, he painted, together with the above-said Battista [Zelotti], in fresco, the room of the Magistrate da Porto in Thiene near Vicenza;[1] and subsequently, with the same, various works, made with draughtsmanship, judgment, and good manner at the Soranza.[2] At Maser, near Asolo in the region of Treviso, he painted the beautiful house of Daniele Barbaro, patriarch-elect of Aquileia.[3] In Verona, in the refectory of San Nazaro, monastery of the Black Friars [Benedictines], he painted in a large picture on canvas the supper hosted by Simon the leper for the Lord, when the

1. Destroyed 2. Much damaged fragments of the frescoes survive in the Duomo of Castelfranco, the Museo Civico in Vicenza, the Seminario Patriarcale in Venice and in private collections. 3. Still in situ.

*Opposite: Architectural decoration, Villa Barbaro at Maser, ca. 1560*

sinner threw herself at his feet; with many figures, portraits from life, and the most extraordinary perspectives, and under the table there are two dogs so beautiful that they seem alive and natural, and further away certain cripples outstandingly rendered.[4] And by Paolino's hand in Venice, in the Hall of the Council of Ten is an oval, larger than the others there, and in the middle of the ceiling, as the main one, showing a Jupiter who expels the vices, to signify that that supreme and absolute magistracy expels vices, and punishes evil and corrupt men.[5] The same painted the ceiling or true stage of the church of San Sebastiano, which is the most extraordinary work, and the altarpiece for the main chapel with certain paintings which are an ornament to it, and in a similar fashion the organ shutters, all of which are truly most praiseworthy paintings.[6] In the Hall of the Great Council he painted in a large picture Frederick Barbarossa who approaches the pope, with a good number of figures in various clothes and costumes, and all most beautiful and truly representative of the courts of a pope and an emperor and a Venetian senate, with many gentlemen and senators of that

4. Galleria Sabauda, Turin 5. Central canvas now in the Musée du Louvre, Paris, the rest still in situ 6. Still in situ

Republic portrayed from life: and altogether, this work is such in its size, draughtsmanship, and beautiful and varied attitudes, that it is deservedly praised by everyone.[7] After this narrative Paolino painted in certain rooms, which are used by the said Council of Ten, the ceilings with figures in oil, which are in strong foreshortening, and are most remarkable.[8] Likewise he painted, on the way to San Maurizio from San Moisè, in fresco the façade of the house of a merchant, which was the most beautiful work; but the sea-air is consuming it slowly.[9] For Camillo Trevisan in Murano he painted a loggia and a room in fresco, which were highly praised:[10] and in San Giorgio Maggiore in Venice he painted at the head of a large room the wedding at Cana in Galilee on canvas in oil; which was a marvellous work in size, number of figures, and variety of costumes, and invention; and, if I remember well, one can see there more than a hundred and fifty heads, all different and painted with great care.[11] The Procurators of Saint Mark's commissioned from the same man to paint certain corner tondi, which are in the ceiling of

7. Destroyed by fire in 1577 8. Two of the central canvases now in the Musée du Louvre, Paris, the rest still in situ. 9. Destroyed 10. The much damaged and partly detached frescoes are in situ and in the Musée du Louvre, Paris. 11. Musée du Louvre, Paris

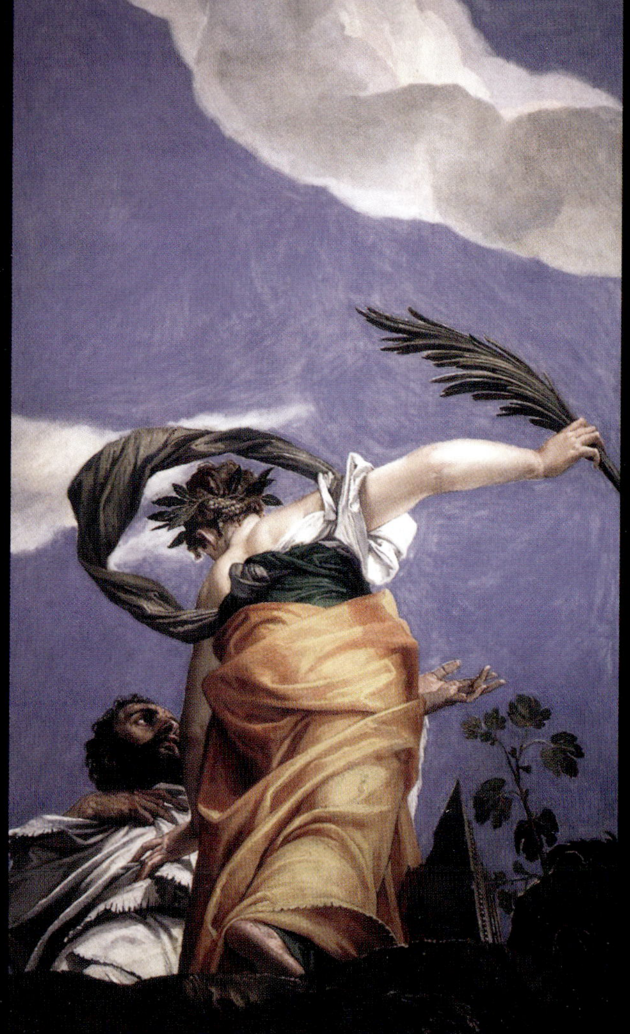

the Library of Saint Mark's, which was left to the Signoria by Cardinal Bessarion with an enormous treasure of Greek books. And because the said lords, when they begun to have the said library painted, promised, to the one who would work the best in painting it, a prize of honour, on top of the ordinary price, the paintings were divided amongst the best painters that were then in Venice. When the work was finished, after having considered carefully the painting of the said pictures, a gold chain was placed around Paolino's neck, as the one who was judged to have worked better than all the others: and the painting that gave the victory and prize of honour, was the one, where Music is depicted; in which are painted three most beautiful young women, one of whom, who is the most beautiful, plays a large bass-viol, looking down to the instrument's handle, and paying the greatest attention to the sound with her ear and personal disposition and voice; of the other two, one plays a lute, and the other sings from a book. Next to the women is a Cupid without wings, who plays a harpsichord, demonstrating that from Music Love is born, or that Love is always in the company of

*Opposite: The Triumph of Virtue over Vice, 1554-6, a ceiling painting from the Doge's Palace*

Music; and because he never leaves her, he painted him without wings. In the same picture he painted Pan, god, according to the poets, of the shepherds, with certain flutes made out of the bark of trees, consecrated to him, almost as vows, by the shepherds who had been victorious with their music-making.[12] Paolino painted two other pictures in the same place: in one is Arithmetic with certain philosophers dressed in an ancient fashion; and in the other Honour, to whom, being enthroned, sacrifices are offered and royal crowns are presented.[13] But because this youth is exactly approaching the prime of his work, and is not even thirty-two years old, for the time being I will not say anything more about him.

12 Still in situ. 13 Still in situ.

# RAFFAELE BORGHINI

## *Life of Paolo Caliari Veronese, Painter*

*from*

*The "Riposo" of Raffaele Borghini,*
*in which*
*Painting and Sculpture are discussed,*
*the most famous Works are mentioned,*
*and the main elements of those Arts*
*are taught*

1584

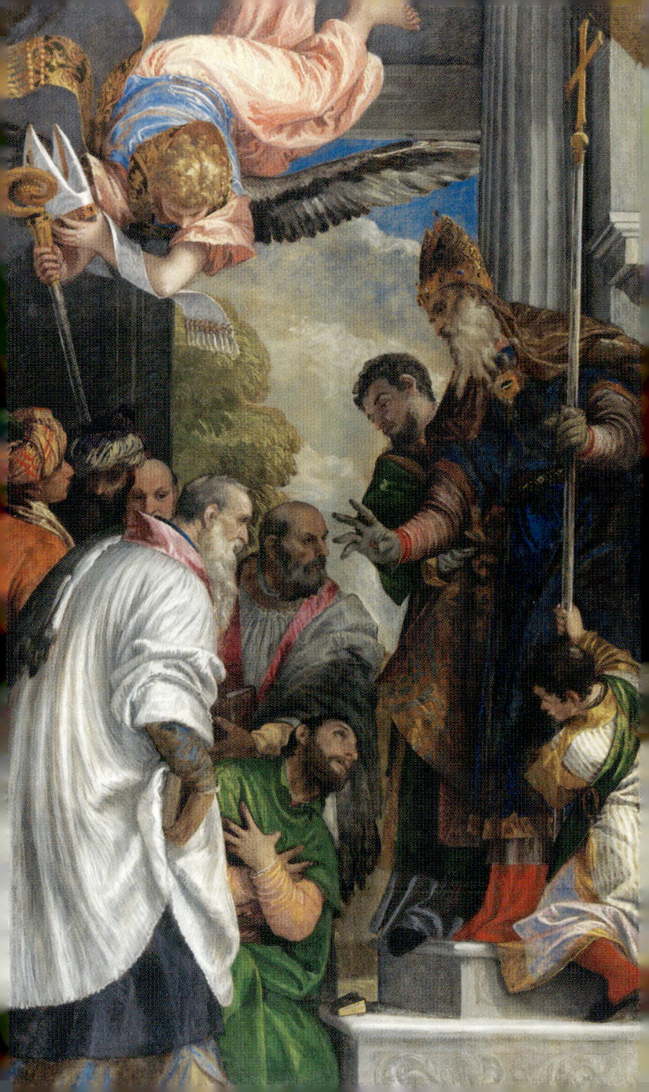

Also in Venice Paolo Calier Veronese is renowned, who was the son of Gabriele the sculptor, & learnt the art of painting from Antonio Badile Veronese his uncle.[1] He has produced many works; but I will mention only those of which I have heard. In San Benedetto in Mantua he painted three highly praised altarpieces for the black friars [Benedictines]:[2] & in Sant'Andrea in the same city an altarpiece with Saint Anthony beaten by the devil, which work he painted in competition with many others, that are there, and has been considered the best.[3] In Verona in the church of San Giorgio there are two altarpieces by his hand, the one on the high altar representing the martyrdom of Saint Laurence,[4] and the one where a miracle of Saint Barnabas can be seen.[5] In San Lorenzo of the Black Friars in the refectory there is a large painting made by him, which represents the

1. Badile was not Veronese's uncle. 2. National Gallery, London, and Chrysler Museum of Art, Norfolk, Virginia. The third was destroyed in a fire in 1836. 3. Musée des Beaux-Arts, Caen. In fact painted for the cathedral, not Sant'Andrea. 4. Still in situ. In fact a Martyrdom of Saint George. 5. Musée des Beaux-Arts, Rouen

*Opposite: The Consecration of St Nicholas, 1562, one of the altarpieces made for San Benedetto in Po, near Mantua*

supper of Christ with the apostles, and there is the Magdalene, who anoints his feet.[6] In Vicenza at the Madonna del Monte in the refectory of the Servite friars he painted a picture of the last supper of the Saviour with the apostles,[7] which was much appreciated, also like an altarpiece in Santa Corona of the Adoration of the Magi.[8] In Santa Giustina in Padua the altarpiece on the high altar is by his hand, which can be seen in print:[9] and in San Francesco in the same city another altarpiece of the Ascension of Our Lord.[10] In Venice these are the works painted by him: in the refectory of the Black Friars of San Giorgio a painting of Christ's miracle of transforming water into wine:[11] in the refectory of the Servite Friars another painting,[12] and an altarpiece in the church:[13] in Santi Giovanni e Paolo a large painting of a feast made by an apostle,[14] and in the church an altarpiece of a dead Christ:[15] in the Library of Saint Mark's he painted in competition with other painters three pictures,[16] and he won as a prize from the Procurators a

6. Galleria Sabauda, Turin. In fact for the church of San Nazaro, not San Lorenzo. 7. Still in situ 8. Still in situ 9. Still in situ 10. Still in situ 11. Musée du Louvre, Paris 12. Musée National du Château, Versailles 13. Stolen and replaced by a Padovanino, now in the Accademia, Venice. 14 Accademia, Venice 15. Hermitage, Saint Petersburg 16. Still in situ.

gold chain: and in the Doge's Palace, where the council meets he painted the ceiling,[17] and a large painting over the doge's throne,[18] which are works highly praised by everyone. In the Hall of the Council of Ten the majority of paintings are by his hand: & he painted two ceilings, where the three major Chiefs are,[19] and now that the ceiling of the Hall of the Great Council has been renovated he has painted three pictures worthy of praise on the side of the doge's tribune.[20] In the sacristy of San Zaccaria he painted an altarpiece,[21] & one at Castello in the church of the patriarch;[22] the one of the high altar in Santa Caterina:[23] one in San Giuliano of the Merceria:[24] One in the sacristy of San Francesco della Vigna,[25] and two in the church:[26] and in San Sebastiano in the middle of two very large paintings the altarpiece of the high altar.[27] He then painted many pictures for princes, and for distinguished people, such as four most beautiful paintings for the Most Serene Carlo Duke of Savoy, in the first there is the Queen of Sheba, who meets Solomon,[28] in the

17. Still in situ 18. Still in situ 19. Two of the central canvases now in the Musée du Louvre, Paris, the rest still in situ. 20. Still in situ 21. Accademia, Venice 22. Still in situ 23. Accademia, Venice 24. Still in situ 25. Destroyed 26. Still in situ 27. Still in situ. 28. Galleria Sabauda, Turin

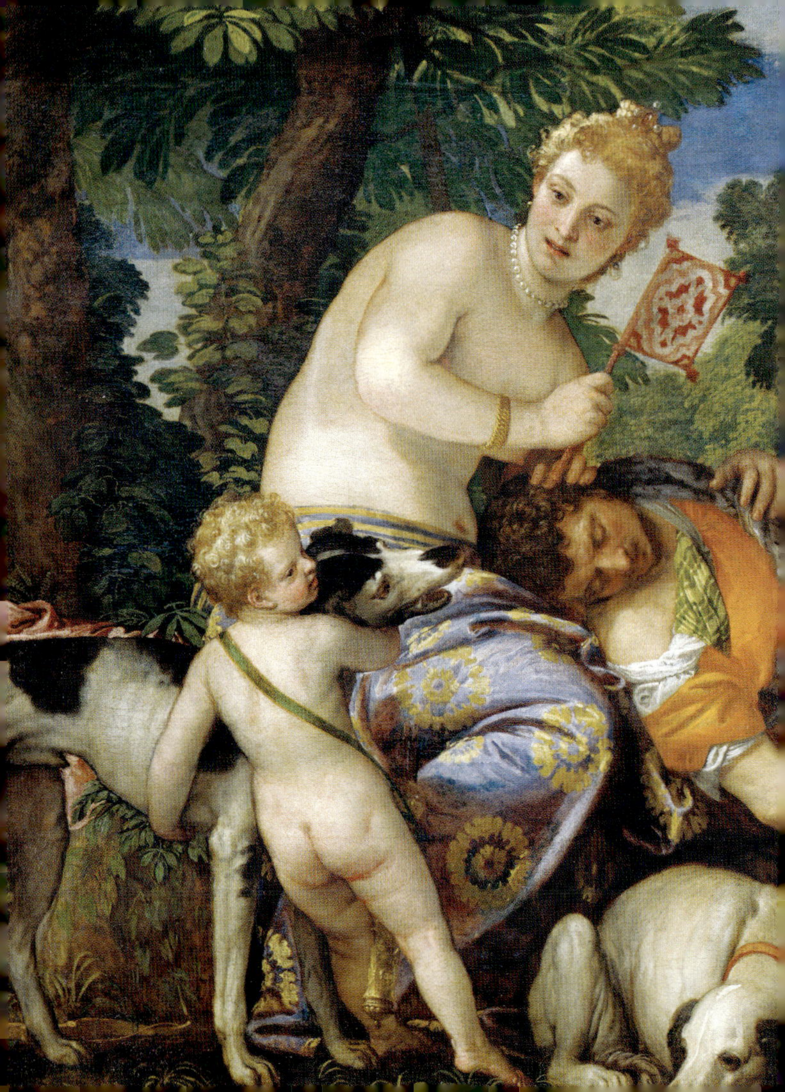

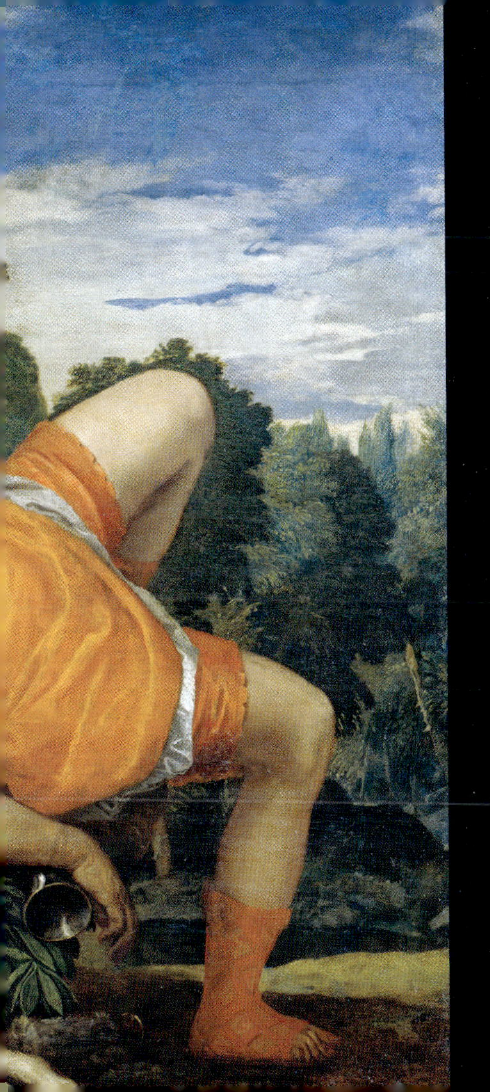

*Venus and Adonis, c. 1580*

second the Adoration of the Magi, in the third David with the head of Goliath, and in the fourth Judith with the head of Holofernes; for the emperor he also painted two, in one of which is Venus, and Mars, and Cupid, who weeps: and in the other a Venus, who arranges her hair, and Cupid holds the mirror, both painted truly with good grace. Recently he painted two most beautiful pictures, one of Procris,[29] and the other of Adonis sleeping in Venus's lap,[30] with life-size figures. Paolo is now fifty-two years old, and he has not ceased from painting continuously to great advantage.

29. Musée des Beaux-Arts, Strasbourg
30. Museo del Prado, Madrid

CARLO RIDOLFI

# *Life of Paolo Caliari Veronese, Painter*

*from*
*The Marvels of Art,*
*or,*
*the Lives of the illustrious Painters of Venice and the Republic*
1648

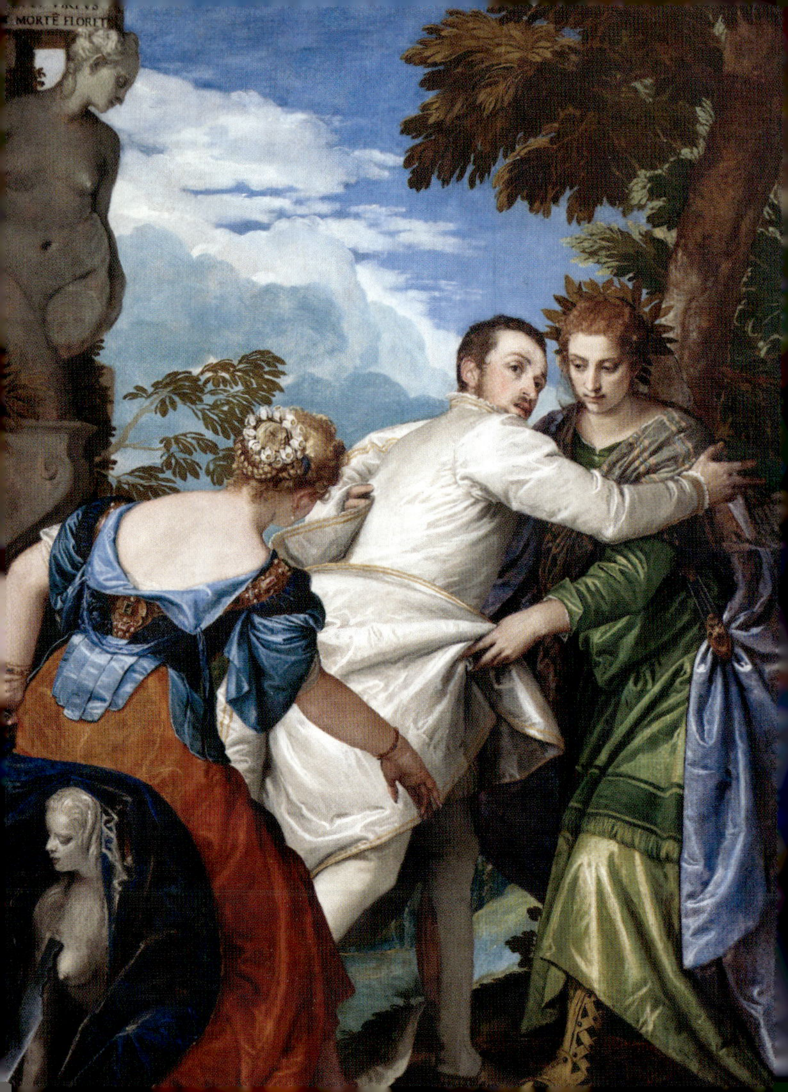
MORTE FLORET

The eloquence of orators or the hyperbole of poets are not enough fully to explain the beauty of painting, which being nothing other than a marvellous compendium of the effects of nature (whereby the eye being fixed on it will wander deluded among its fictions), when one tries suitably to talk about it every style is confused and every vein of inspiration is impoverished. As a matter of fact, it is even more surprising to consider that in the beginning man had no other master than the great painting of the world, on which the supreme artist God painted all things, and that man dared to emulate divine actions with little lines and mute colours, so that he too, through art, gave flight to the birds, flickering to the fish, growth to the plants and motion to the animals.

The brush of an industrious painter here proves the point, because amongst the tapestries of painted gardens he makes roses, amaranths and violets sprout, and at the summit of mountains laurels, cypresses and olive trees. He colours the bright dawn and the sun, which, dissolving the vermilion clouds, gleefully rises again with its golden mane to illuminate the sky.

*Opposite: The Choice between Virtue and Vice, c. 1565*

He shapes a stormy sea, which with its haughty waves wages war on the stars; and among the paths of liquefied silver here and there reveals to our appreciative gaze Venuses, Galateas, Graces and Cupids. He embroiders the bodies of animals, infuses brightness in gold, splendour in gems, and in a commendable way he represents every extraordinary impression which can be admired in creation.

Here he is emulating further every human invention, while in the small surface of a panel or a canvas he raises colossi, builds palaces, erects temples and obelisks; and with lifelike appearances he displays the massacres, fires and the vicissitudes of worldly things from past times; and in addition to depicting the variety of bodies, he expresses in human faces joy, disdain, happiness, pain and all the soul's passions, acting on some occasions as an eloquent painter and on others as a painting orator. In conclusion Painting is that mirror in which all the works of the Creator, all that the amplitude of the earth holds at its bosom and all that the circuit of the sky surrounds can be seen and summarized.

But because one cannot do justice to such a worthy subject with words, the most satisfactory praise

*Opposite: Wisdom and Strength, c. 1565*

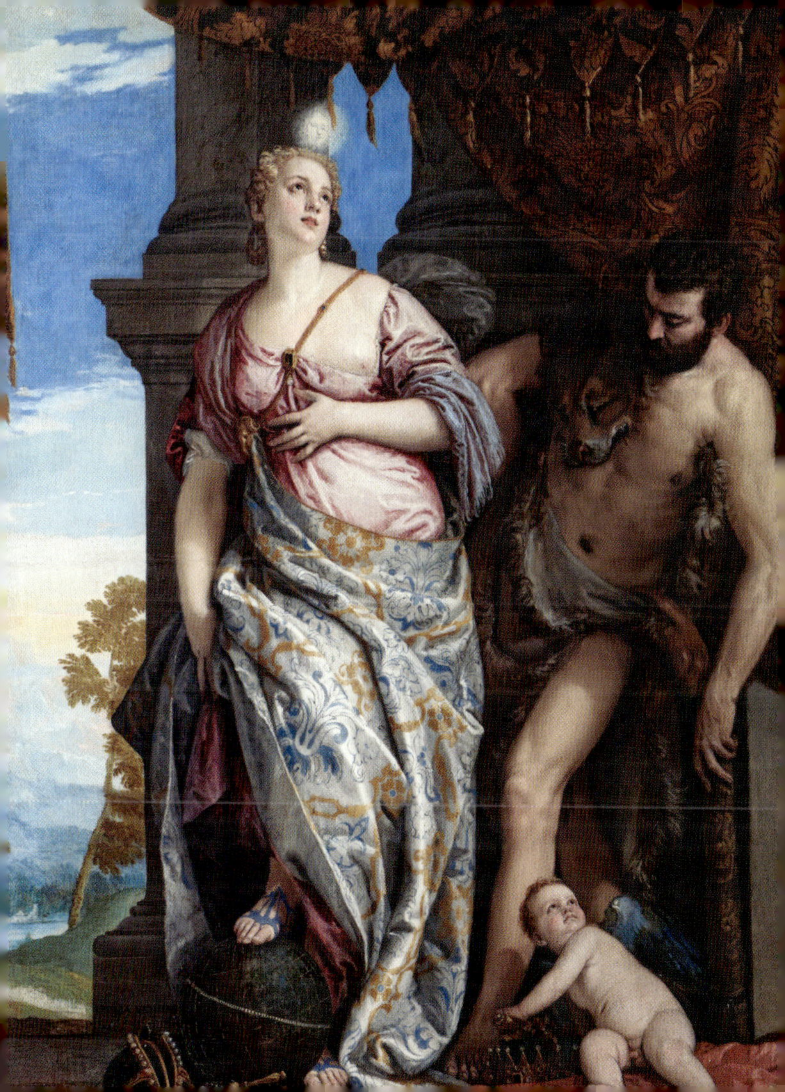

one can pay is to contemplate it while keeping silent, and to demonstrate its beauties with the works of excellent artists; and in particular with those of Paolo, agreeing with all the opinions of those who understand these things that he achieved the first aim of Art in working in a way never practised by other painters, as in his paintings you can admire outlandish and majestic gods, grave characters, matrons full of graces and charm, kings richly adorned, the diversity of draperies, various military spoils, ornate architecture, joyous plants, beautiful animals and many of these curiosities that can well satisfy the eye of the viewer with the most pleasant entertainment, and that therefore he is most famous in the ranks of the most celebrated painters of the modern age.

Nor do we presume to burnish so much worth with these inky characters, but only with the pen to summarize the honours of that man.

Paolo was born in Verona, illustrious city of Lombardy, famous for its antiquities, for its happy seat, for the outstanding arches and theatres, imitators of the noblest buildings in Rome. Through it flows the proud river Adige which, like the storied Tiber, irrigates the green edge of its delightful hills with its speedy course, and the city is famous not only for its martial merits, but also for those of wise

Minerva, because it boasts of having produced this famous painter as an epitome of its greatness.

Now Paolo was born in the year 1530 to bring more honour to his homeland and beauty to the world.[1] His father was Gabriele Caliari, citizen of Verona and sculptor, who taught him as a boy the principles of his art, training him to make terracotta models; but seeing that he was better suited to paint than to sculpt he put him under the guidance of his uncle Antonio Badile, who worked in Verona as a successful painter.[2] A panel by Badile's hand can be seen in the left nave of the church of San Nazaro in which the Virgin is represented on the clouds with the child in her lap, and below certain bishop saints and a boy who holds a book with other figures, and in San Bernardino the resurrected Lazarus; from these one can understand the origin of that gentle style which was increased in beauty and nobility by Paolino, as he was then affectionately known.[3]

He lived for some time in his uncle's house, where his knowledge increased with age ; and he produced marvels first in drawing and then in colouring. His mind was endowed with those elements that one

1. In fact Paolo was born in 1528. 2. Badile was not Veronese's uncle.
3. Paintings still in SS. Nazaro e Celso and San Bernardino

looks for in a good painter, quick apprehension, endurance of hard work; he could memorize everything he learnt, was of a noble genius and made nothing whose idea did not exhale grace and pleasure; to prove that in the green April of his years he give birth with flowers to the most jocund fruits.

He started then to produce work on his own, to his father's delight, because worthy parents do not desire anything else for their children than to see them setting out on the road to honour. Thus he painted in San Fermo in Verona a small altarpiece with Our Lady sitting with two saints;[4] in San Bernardino, in front of the Lazarus by his master, Our Lord, healing Saint Peter's mother-in-law;[5] and in the street two well-coloured figures can also be found.[6] From these beginnings it was already possible to foresee his future prominence.

Brought to Mantua at this time by Cardinal Ercole Gonzaga, together with Domenico Riccio known as Brusasorci, Battista dal Moro, and Paolo Farinati, young painters from Verona, to paint the

4. Also known as the Pala Bevilacqua Lazise, Museo di Castelvecchio, Verona. 5. Lost since 1697. 6. Destroyed

*Opposite: The Virgin and Child with Saints and Donors (Pala Bevilacqua Lazise), ca. 1546*

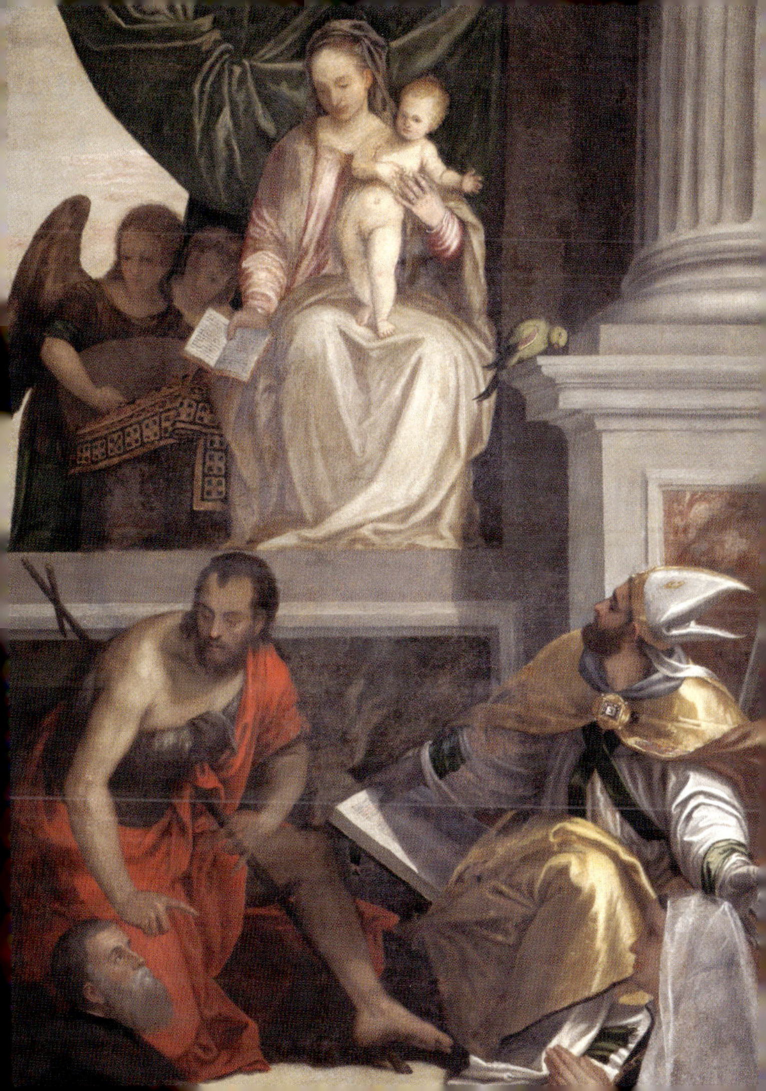

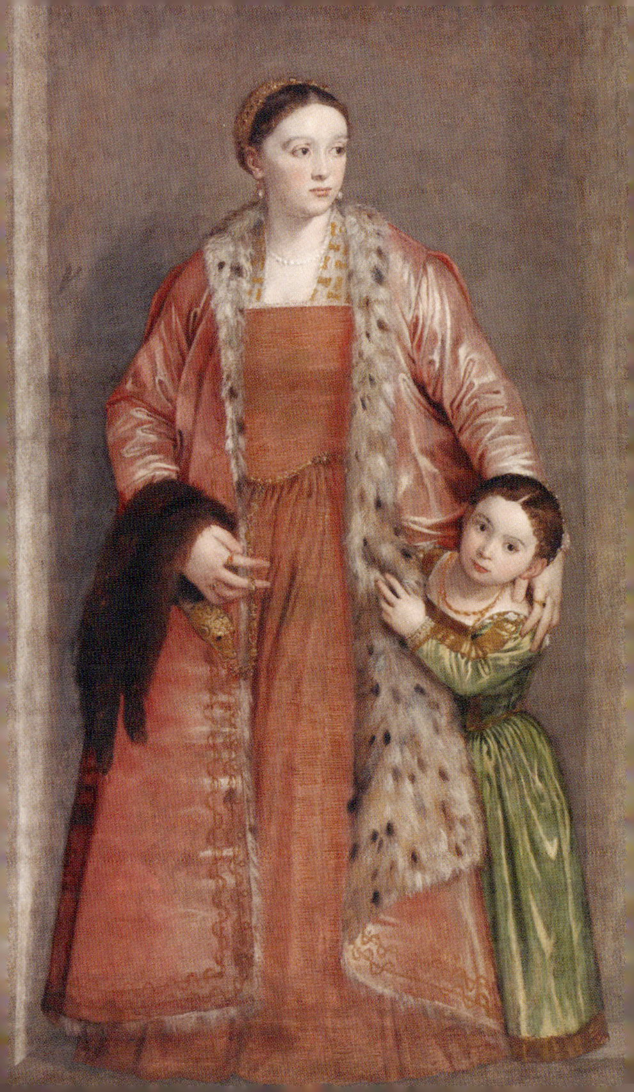

altarpieces of the Duomo, Paolo painted in his Saint Anthony Abbot beaten with a stick by a demon and misled by another in the guise of a woman, and he surpassed in merit his competitors.[7]

Having been rewarded by the cardinal he returned to Verona, spending a short time in copying the painting by Raphael belonging to the Counts Canossa, which is still kept in the same palace;[8] and in other private works. But not being particularly happy, finding nothing other than misfortune (confirming in fact what Christ had said, that no prophet is honoured in his homeland), he thought of improving his luck under a more favourable sky. (Plants moved to a different soil often improve in grace and beauty.) And it did not take long before he followed his intention with deeds, and he went to Thiene near Vicenza, where in the houses of the Counts Da Porto he painted in the *sala* in fresco men and women who play at a table, a banquet of knights and ladies, a hunt and a ball, all flanked by figures in grisaille,

7. Musée des Beaux-Arts, Caen 8. Raphael's *Holy Family* (known as La Perla) is now in the Museo del Prado, Madrid. Veronese's copy was still recorded in the Canossa Palace in 1888, but is now lost.

*Opposite: Livia da Porto Thiene and her daughter Deidamia, 1552*

and in the frames he painted cartouches, putti and festoons.[9]

Above the door of a large room are Pallas and Mercury resting on a pediment; and on the walls are four scenes, of Mucius Scævola who burns his hand as a punishment for having killed the secretary instead of King Porsena; of Sophonisba in front of Massinissas, who then married her to save her from being paraded in triumph; of Mark Anthony at the banquet with Cleopatra with a regal setting and a cortège of servants; and of Xerxes enthroned, to whom the people of Greece bring gifts in tribute; and a frieze all around of youths and festoons. In the doors he painted huntsmen in trompe-l'œil and near a fireplace Venus and Vulcan. Battista Zelotti, his fellow pupil, also partly collaborated on this project, and because he was so similar in his manner, he worked on Paolo's paintings in a way that could not be distinguished from Paolo's, to prove that their works could pass as being by the same hand. And some say that Paolo also used Antonio Fasolo from Vicenza who was very young at the time and was studying from his paintings.

Having moved to Fanzolo, a village near Treviso, he worked again in fresco with Battista in the house

9. Destroyed

of the Emo family, and painted above the door of the loggia Ceres surrounded by rural implements, and on the sides Jupiter in the guise of Diana with Callisto, and Callisto beaten by Juno.[10]

In one of the rooms it is possible to see in three compartments the story of Adonis. In a *camerino* the story of Io divided into four compartments, and in another room the personifications of Painting, Sculpture and the Liberal Arts, in the ceiling of the sala the Muses and slaves tied to the bases of columns painted as a decoration.

Having completed the said works and others which are scattered around those villages, Battista left for Vicenza to paint in the Monte di Pietà, while Paolo travelled to Venice, as his own virtue could not obtain any progress if exposed in the wilderness, so he intended to work in a more conspicuous place which would welcome its beauty, because as someone has said:

> What is beauty worth if not seen? And even if seen,
> Not admired? And even if admired
> Admired by one only person?[11]

10. Not by Veronese. All frescoes in the villa are by Zelotti.
11. Boiardo, *Pastor Fido*, Act I, Scene 3

Having therefore established his home in Venice he had the material to let his worth be known; and even though one could see the unique paintings of Titian in that city, and those of Palma il Vecchio, and at the time the flower of Tintoretto's art, he did not miss precious opportunities.

Thus Father Bernardo Torlioni, the prior of San Sebastiano, his loving fellow countryman, commissioned from him the ceiling of the sacristy, where he painted the Coronation of the Virgin with the Evangelists around it.[12] But the putti placed in those roundels, who hold books and two cartouches, on one of which is written: *Coronam in capite tuo accipe* [Accept the crown upon your head] and on the other: *accipe dignitatem & coronam æternam*, [accept the honour and the eternal crown] were by the hand of one of his pupils.

As the work was liked, Torlioni gave Paolo the ceiling of the church to paint, which had been recently renovated, and that was divided in good order in two ovals and a square in the middle surrounded by other smaller spaces.[13]

In the first oval he painted Esther, beautiful and graceful, brought by the servants in front of King

12. Still in situ 13. Still in situ

Ahasuerus, and next to her is her uncle Mordecai who is warning her to keep her origins hidden.

In the middle Esther is crowned by that same Ahasuerus, taking the place of Queen Vashti, as the latter had not obeyed him, and then beautiful Esther obtains through her sweet prayers the liberation of her people and honours for the uncle, because where uncommon beauty reigns, everything is obeyed, so as the poet sang:

> Artibus innumeris mens oppugnatur amantum,
> Ut lapis æquoreis undique pulsus aquis.*

And in the other oval, which frames the square picture, Mordecai is brought riding a large horse across the city by Haman, and is acclaimed as a friend of the king, and in that way he is rewarded for having uncovered the eunuchs' conspiracy.

Fortune often shakes destiny. Haman, earlier revered as the Lord of Persia, now becomes the groom of a slave, and is made into an example of those hateful courtiers, who at the height of their prominence experience a precipitous fall from power. Fortune, when it shines, is made out of glass. In the

*With various arts they storm a lover's mind,/Like some bleak rock expos'd to waves and wind. Ovid, *Remedy of Love*

remaining spaces Paolo divided balustrades and putti above festoons, figures in grisaille and coloured in yellow earth.

Once the paintings were uncovered, not only because of the novelty of the structure, but for the remarkable works of Paolo (as similar beauties had not been seen in the ceilings of churches before), many people went to admire the paintings, giving immortal praise to their author. And this was the reason why those priests, without waiting any further, wished him to continue to paint the vault of the main chapel, in which he frescoed Our Lady ascending to Heaven surrounded by many angels; and at the top of the tribune he depicted God the Father and angels above balconies, who are making merry with various musical instruments, and the Doctors of the Church in the spandrels, and the Evangelists in two lunettes.[14]

He painted two scenes in the choir of the friars: one of Saint Sebastian in front of Diocletian, confessing to be a knight of Christ; but this scenes having been ruined was then covered by an oil painting by Paolo of the same subject. In the other scene the knightly Saint is beaten by henchmen with sticks.[15] Above the seats he painted in two niches in grisaille

14. Destroyed 15. Both damaged frescoes still in situ

the apostles Saints Peter and Paul and other prophets, and figures around them in grisaille, Sibyls and coloured angels who play music and sing, two executioners who are firing arrows and Saint Sebastian on the other side, and it was all divided by twisted columns which were decorated with reliefs and pretty adornments. Above the arches of the chapels he divided the apostles and two prophets on each side of the organ, the Annunciation in the arch of the main chapel and Sibyls over those of the two neighbouring smaller chapels. And when he painted those works he was only twenty seven years old.

Recognized henceforth as one of the city's worthy painters he produced many paintings in oil and following the demand of patrons started again to paint in fresco. Having gone to the Villa Soranza near Castelfranco he painted in the loggia of that building, columns, landscapes, the seasons and youths with different fruits in their hands.[16] He depicted in lunettes Mars and Venus, Jupiter and Juno, Mercury and Pallas with other gods, and on the ceiling youths in compartments, and at the head above the balustrade he placed two seated men, one of them

16. Much damaged fragments of the frescoes survive in the Duomo of Castelfranco, the Museo Civico in Vicenza, the Seminario Patriarcale in Venice and in private collections.

with an old-fashioned coat and hat which is said to be a self-portrait of Paolo in the act of reading, and he also painted there two most natural dogs.

In the middle of the ceiling of the *sala* he depicted a sky with gods, and figures all around the vault; and on the walls scenes and sacrifices surrounded by female figures in grisaille, and other over-doors.

In one of the rooms there is a most natural looking vine with small birds, in the shape of a tribune, and in the small arches are heads painted to look like bronze. On the walls there is Alexander who cuts with his sword the Gordian knot, and the women of Darius in front of that same Alexander, who orders that they should be treated like queens.

In the second room there are, as in the other, Virtues painted over the doors, and figures in grisaille in the compartments, and they are fine works by Paolo. And here it is said that Zelotti, who as we have said was his fellow pupil, also worked.

Around that same time Paolo went to Maser, a village near Asolo in the area of Treviso, having been called by Daniele Barbaro, patriarch-elect of Aquileia, and Marcantonio his brother, who liked his new and delightful style. There in their palace built

*Opposite: Servant opening a door: decoration at the Villa Barbaro at Maser, c. 1560*

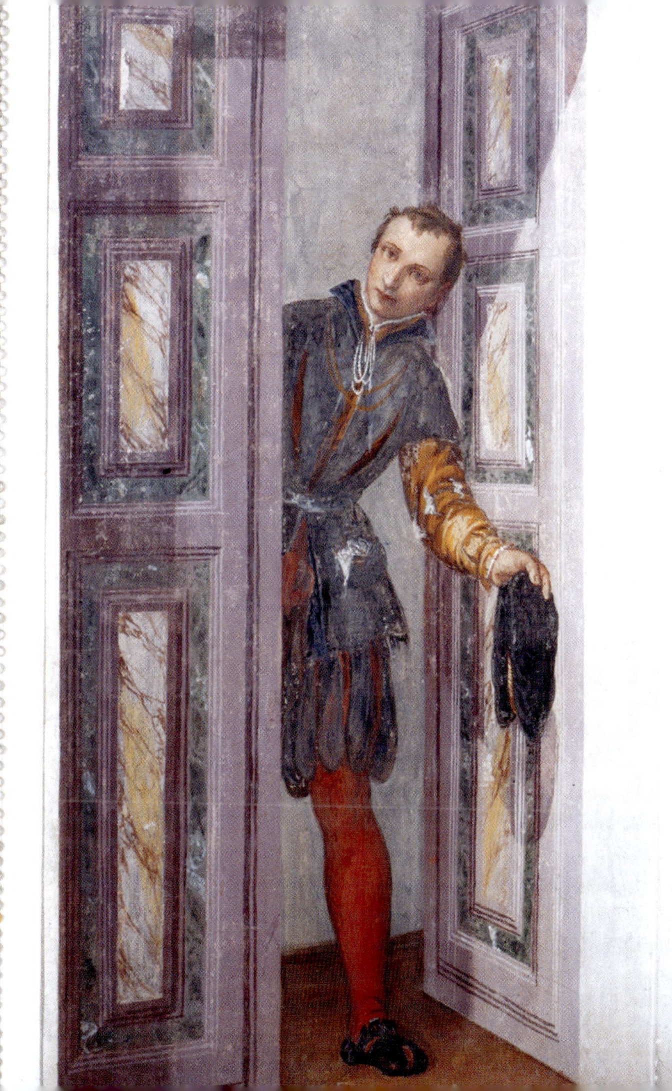

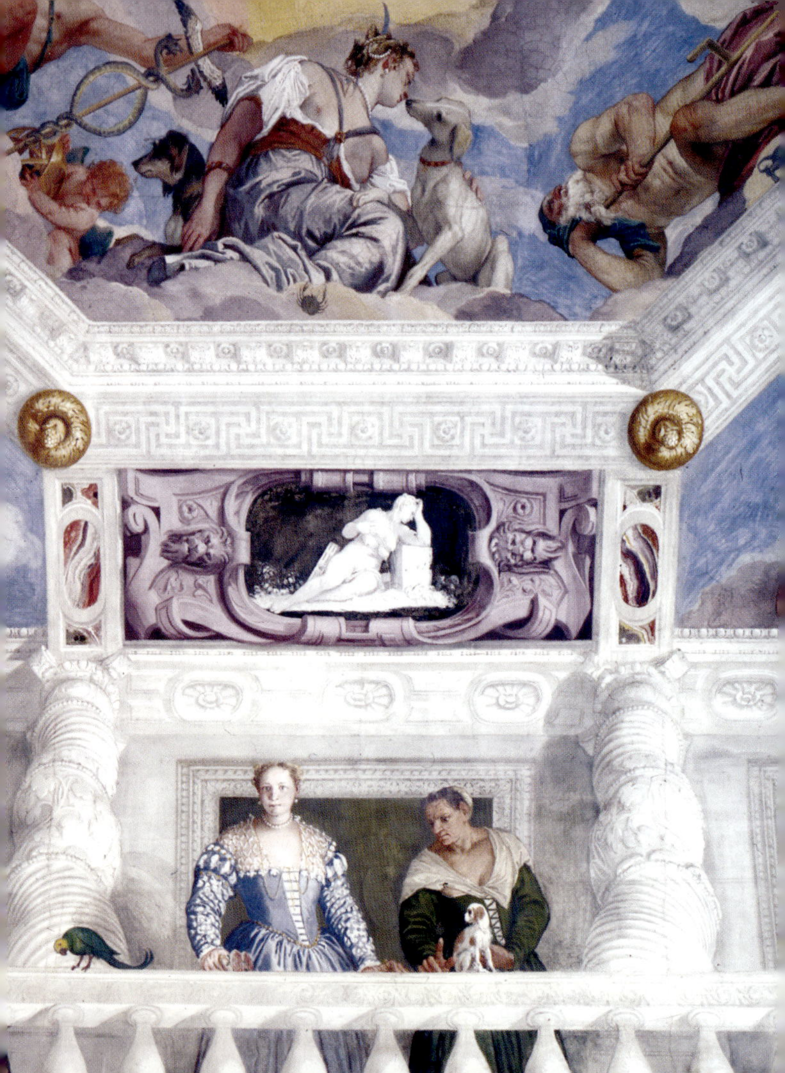

on the models by Andrea Palladio, the famous architect, he painted new marvels.[17]

In the cross-shaped *sala* he represented the Muses with their instruments, architectures, pleasing landscapes and military spoils. In certain false doors he portrayed valets and grooms, and in the ceilings festoons and leafy branches. On one side of the *sala* he represented noble architectures, and above a balcony with ladies, and others with books and musical instruments in their hands, who look up to the sky, where the planets are depicted with their symbols.

He further arranged round the two rooms columns with satyrs painted as if made out of bronze, above the doors coloured figures which represent Nobility, Dominion, Honour, Magnificence, and other similar personifications alluding to the dignity of that family; and on the ceilings are Juno, Ceres, Flora, Vertumnus and a very smooth nude Bacchus who is squeezing a bunch of grapes, to point to the quantity of flowers, wheat and fruits that are plentiful in that enchanting place, and to these paintings he gave such grace and nobility that they appear

17. Still in situ

*Opposite: Sala dell'Olimpo (detail), Villa Barbaro at Maser, ca. 1560*
*Overleaf: Ceiling of the Stanza di Bacco, Villa Barbaro at Maser, ca. 1560*

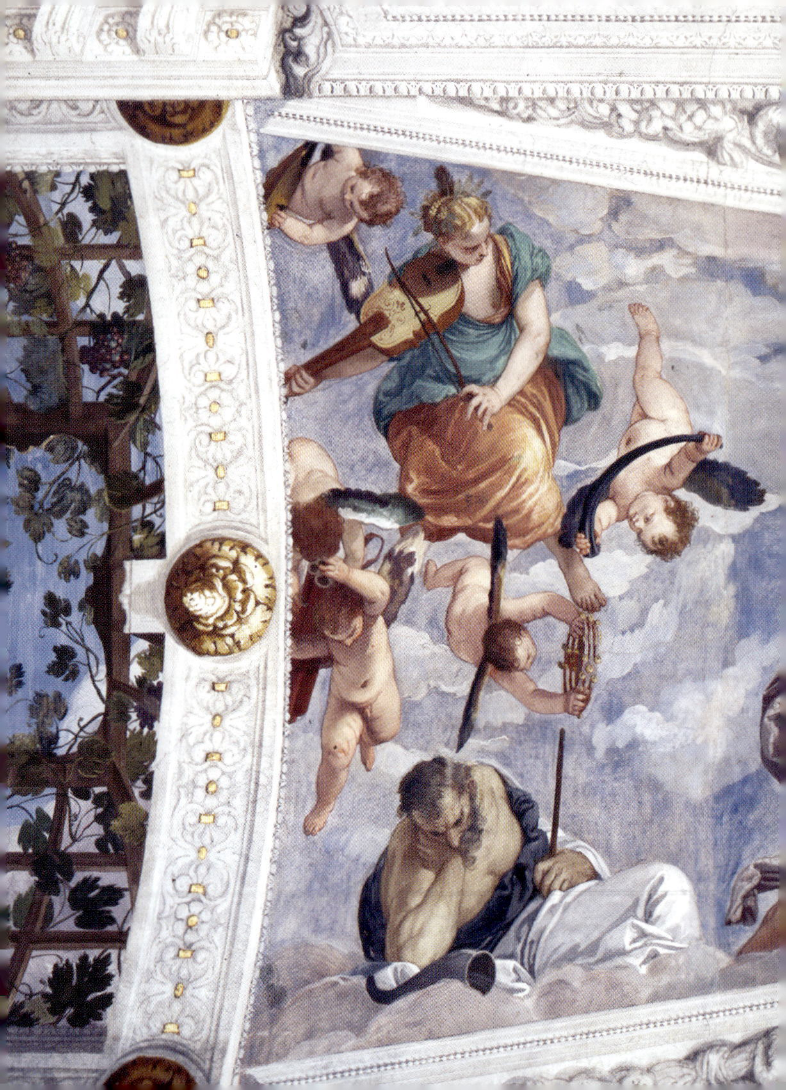

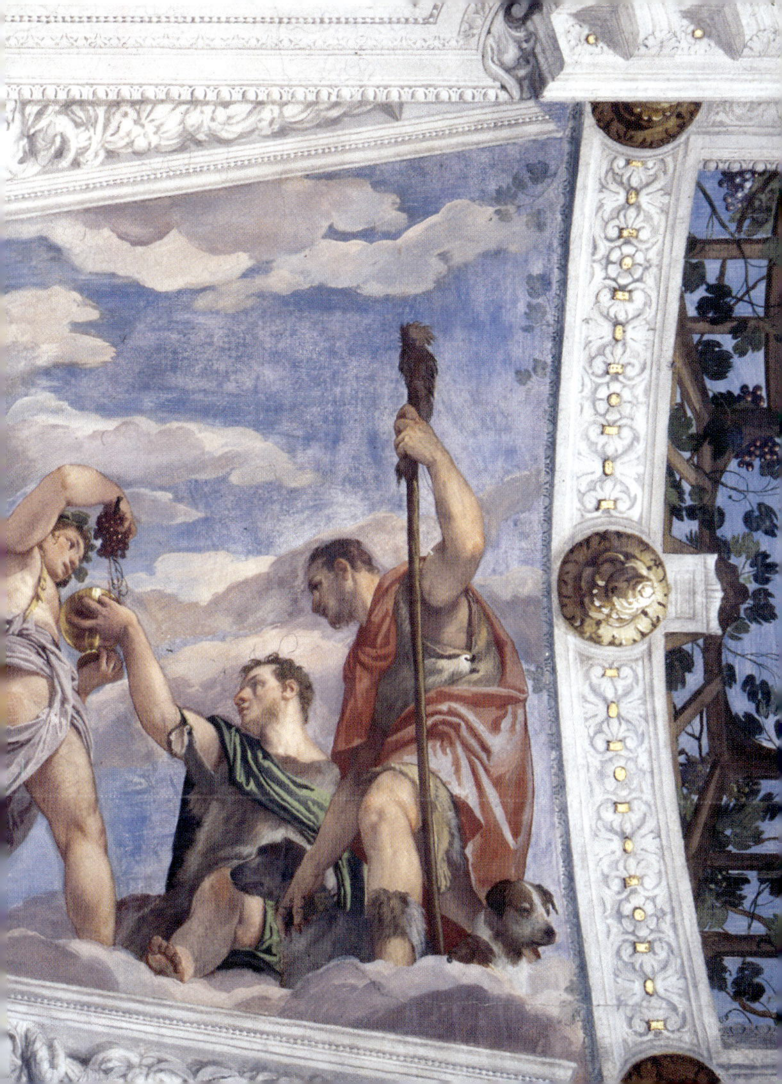

to be celestial things. And he also depicted there certain devotional images in feigned paintings.

In the side towards the *peschiera* near the hill he painted certain small scenes and Peace in the middle of a ceiling, and there are also figures in stucco, which Marcantonio Barbaro used himself to sculpt for pleasure. And so these lords, for the great service received from Paolo, always protected him and helped bring on his good fortune. Even though it is noble by Nature, virtue cannot make itself distinguished to the eyes of mortals, who fix their eyes where gold glitters most, if the great with their power do not help her, as everyone easily agrees with their views. Gems advance in state in the hands of lords, whose opinions are always followed by inferior people.

Soon after he also painted in fresco in Venice, in the house of Bellavite overlooking Campo San Maurizio, four painted scenes, two in grisaille of episodes from Roman history, where Marcius Coriolanus reconciliates himself again with his homeland, following the prayers of his mother Veturia, and was subsequently killed by the Volsci.[18] At the top are two youths sitting over festoons, and below the windows he painted coloured cartouches

18. Destroyed

and cameos; and among them others in grisaille with satyrs around; and below the windows of the mezzanines cuirasses and instruments of war also in grisaille. Standing above the modillions are two outstanding figures painted as if in bronze, who represent Prudence and Minerva with olive branches and ears of wheat in their hands, to signify that the owner had built the house with the money he had made from oil and grain.

Since at this time some of the old paintings in the Doge's Palace were ruined, some were given to paint to Orazio, the son of Titian, and some to Tintoretto: so, because he had become known through his works at San Sebastiano (and because the Barbaro had promoted his merit for the remarkable works he had done for them at Maser), Paolo was commissioned to paint one of the main scenes in the Hall of the Great Council, in which he represented with great beauty Emperor Frederick I recognizing Octavian as Pope, with many characters in his cortège splendidly dressed, and he portrayed in it from life Luigi Mocenigo, who was Doge, Agostino Barbarigo, who died in the naval battle [Lepanto], Marcantonio Grimani, Antonio Cappello, Girolamo Contarini and Lorenzo Giustiniani, Procurators of Saint Mark's, Abbot Francesco Loredan, Nicolò Zeno and others, and with the inscription:

Alexandrum III Pont. Max. rite creatum &
Octavianum vitio factum
Imper. Feder. Ticinum evocavit. Alex. dicto
eius audiens non fuit.
Itaque Federicus id ægre ferens Octavianum, qui ad
se iit Pont. declaravit ac veneratus est.*

Above two large windows he painted Time, Faith, Patience, and Union with fasces of rods in her hand, an allusion to the preservation of that Republic and the love nourished among the citizens, and because the Catholic religion has always been preserved there. But all of these paintings were destroyed in the fire of the palace in the year 1576.

In the room of the Chiefs of the Council of Ten he painted in the middle of the ceiling an angel, who casts out vice, with women at its feet who are escaping, representing other vices.[19] Innocence and other

* Alexander III, Supreme Pontiff, rightfully elected, and Octavian, illegitimately appointed, were both summoned by the Emperor Frederick to Ticinum [Pavia]. Alexander did not respond to the summons. Frederick taking this ill, declared Octavian, who did come to him, Pope and venerated him.

19. Musée du Louvre, Paris

similar personifications present supplications, accompanied by Time, and protected by that great Magistracy.[20] Around it are symbols representing its authority; but two of those are by another hand; and above the tribune still is a dead Christ supported by angels by Antonello da Messina, which according to this author is worthy of mention.[21]

In the ceiling of the ante-room he painted Saint Mark with a golden crown in his hand, a small angel supports him, and another one holds with beautiful demeanour the book of the Gospels resting on the lion, and in the lower part are the Theological Virtues looking upwards, and in the surrounds in long spaces are Roman triumphs in green earth and figures in grisaille.[22]

But these were, so to speak, small examples of Paolo's virtue and greater things were demonstrated by subsequent events. As a consequence of the competition promoted by Titian (at the request of the Procurators of Saint Mark's) between the most excellent young painters, who were Giuseppe Salviati, Battista Franco, Schiavone, Zelotti and Fratino,

20. Still in situ 21. The painting in the Doge's Palace is signed by Antonello de Saliba, often confused with Antonello da Messina. 22. Central canvas now in the Musée du Louvre, Paris, the rest still in situ.

Paolo was to be among the first, and he was given three tondi to paint for the ceiling of the Library of Saint Mark's towards the Campanile, in which he depicted the following compositions.[23]

In the first he portrayed some beautiful women to represent Music, who are playing lutes and violas while one sings from a book, and with them is Love, because some say that he was the inventor of Music, and because music and songs are a stimulation to loving, hence Menander:

> Musica multis est incitamentum amoris.*

Love is also supposedly born from idleness and human lust, hence Petrarch:

> He was born from idleness and human lust
> Fed by sweet and gentle thoughts,
> Made Lord and God by vain people.

Truly so it is, and Love feeds on delicate food, and is encouraged by scents and lascivious things; lovers make for him delicate cushions of roses, and pamper him with fans of soft feathers, and with the music of the most beautiful and idle girls he takes the most gentle leisure, and as Ovid sang:

* If music be the food of love etc.

23. Still in situ

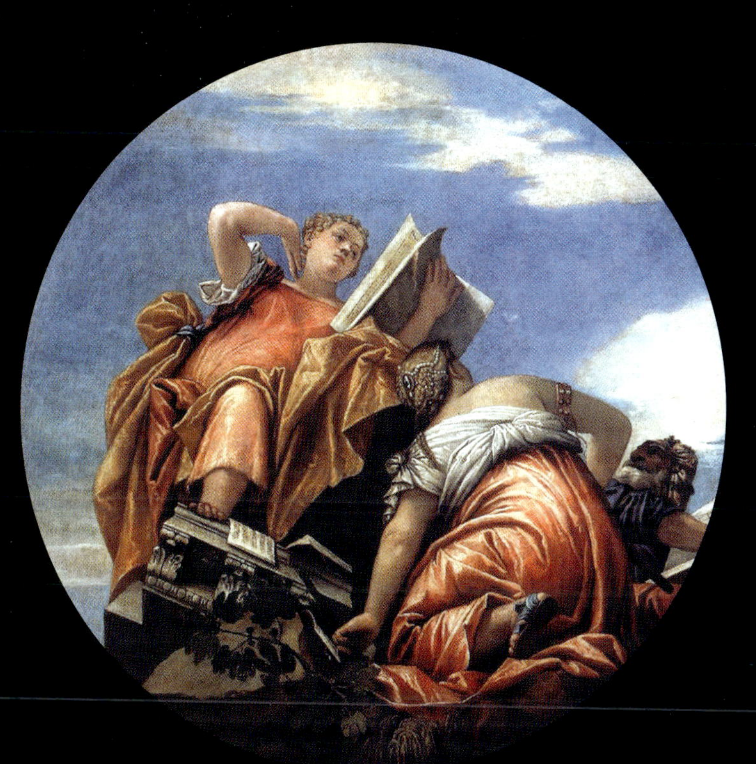

*Music, Astronomy and Deceit, 1556,*
*one of the tondi painted for the Library of St Mark's*

Ergo, ubi visus eris nostra medicabilis arte,
Fac monitis fugias otia prima meis.

Hæc, ut ames faciunt; hæc quæ fecere tuentur;
Hæc funt icundi causa cibusque mali.

Otia si tollas, periere Cupidinis arcus,
Contemptæque iacent & sine luce faces.*

In the second he made two beautiful figures for Geometry and Arithmetic.

And in the third is Honour, who is born from the study of the various disciplines, placed on a pedestal, in front of which are philosophers, historians and poets, who are offering him garlands of flowers, ivy and laurel, which they have won after sleepless nights and hard work, as their scattered seeds yield them only bitter fruits and insipid leaves, about which Stigliano wrote:

I understood the Muses but ill before
Because they are false barren virgins
And the laurel yields none but bitter fruit.

* If therefore you expect to find redress,/In the first place take leave of idleness;/'Tis this that kindl'd first your fond desire,/'Tis this brings fuel to the am'rous fire./Bar idleness, you ruin Cupid's game,/You blunt his arrows, and you quench his flame. Ovid, *Remedy of Love*, translated by John Dryden

I will not plough the sea any longer,
My brow, let us sweat for some other work,
Because it is a meagre prize to encircle you with wreaths.

And because the Procurators had decided to give a sign of particular honour to the one amongst the said painters who had painted the best works, again they asked Titian and Sansovino to be the judges. But because they did not want to be considered partial, they judged well by wanting to ask the competing artists themselves, who having been consulted for their opinion of the works of their competitors (excluding their own), they agreed that Paolo was the winner, and this they reported to the same Procurators, who (in addition to the recognition given to each artist), gave him a gold chain, as a sign of the honour which had flowed from it, which is still in the possession of his grandson Giuseppe Caliari as a precious relic of his glorious ancestor. And it is certain that honour, which flows from virtue, should be better prized than wealth, which depends from fortune alone, as Aristotle claims:

Imperia et opes gloriæ causa expectandæ sunt.*

* Power and wealth are desirable [only] for the glory they bring. Aristotle, *Nicomachean Ethics* for, translated by H. Rackham

Greatness sinks, and the names of those who die without the adornment of virtue are extinguished in deep oblivion, and only the memory of outstanding men remains.

He painted for the church of the Crociferi, in the chapel to the right of the altar, Our Lord adored by the shepherds, where the Virgin wraps Him up in humble bandages.[24]

Subsequently, having gone to Verona to visit his relations, he painted for the Fathers of San Nazaro at the head of their refectory an enclosure of handsome architecture, and two columns on each side covered in vine which hold up a majestic frontispiece, and between them he placed festoons hanging from animal skulls. Above the corners of the painting he depicted two female satyrs, most beautiful in their deformity, and in the middle the banquet of Simon the leper with the Magdalene in the act of anointing the feet of the Saviour, in front of whom is the same Simon, astonished at the action of the generous woman; on the other side of the table is treacherous Judas full of hatred, who complains to the people around them of the waste of the precious ointment, which the loving sinner is pouring over the feet of the Lord.[25]

24. SS. Giovanni e Paolo, Venice 25. Galleria Sabauda, Turin

It is impossible to describe with what gravity that woman appears and how she holds one of Jesus' feet in the tresses of her golden hair, and the rest of her loose locks frames with their golden threads the alabaster of her bosom, and she places her other hand, whiter than untouched snow, covered in roses, over the vase of the precious unguent; and finally her every gesture seems to be accompanied by the Graces in that meek action. There are servants with golden vases and others who are serving food at the banquet, mimes dressed in livery with monkeys, who come to entertain the guests; and nothing is lacking of pageantry or spectacle. This painting was copied in its original size by the author of the present *Lives* and was sent to Flanders to a great patron.

Having returned, Paolo continued to work at San Sebastiano, because those Fathers did not want anyone else but him to paint there, and as the decoration of that church was being renewed, he painted the altarpiece for the main altar, in which he represented Our Lady holding the Child and angels; at the bottom Saint Sebastian tied to a column, Saint Peter and Saint Francis, who is a portrait of the said Father Bernardo.[26]

26. Still in situ

But in the painting of the Purification [of the Virgin] on the organ painted by him in the year 1560 he used stronger colours and demonstrated further excellence.[27] Here is the Virgin with the Child in her virginal arms, and with maternal tenderness she offers him to the old Simeon; the venerable priest kneeling over him adores that God, which he had desired to see for a long time, and indulging his eyes in that joyful sight, he wishes to close them in eternal rest. Around the altar are priests, and Levites holding books, servants with lit torches and incense burners, and a woman in brightly coloured drapery stands to one side with two doves as an offering.

On the inside of the shutters is the pool with many sick people, who are waiting for the angel to move the waters. They are assembled within the colonnades of a portico, which forms a large courtyard drawn with strict perspective, and the main figures placed on the principal plane, and the ones further in the distance diminish in sequence with accurate artifice when seen from the floor of the church.

And even though good painters have become accustomed to using an elevated viewpoint to avoid those wearisome perspective views, and to find room

27. Still in situ

for figures in such paintings, in certain cases they have observed the rules, as Paolo did in this place, to show how well he knew the requirements of these blessed rules. Some good minds labour hard over these things, not thinking about more important things, since architecture should only be used as decoration, and the first place must always be given to the figures, as the most essential part of a composition, so that they do not surpass the narrative in quantity and strength. These observations should be adopted as reasonable practice by the wise artist, through which the eye will be satisfied, as the talent of the painter will be recognized in the unfolding of the narrative, and not in boastful display of science. But forgive me for this digression to satisfy those who desire to understand the reason for every thing.

In front, finally, of the portico is Our Lord, who commands to the lame man to pick up his bed and walk, and if his words of thanksgiving as he prepares to leave cannot be heard, it is the fault of painting, that does not allow the expression of voices. Nor would it be a hyperbole in this place to say that the Graces provided Paolo in this worthy mission with the the purple dye of Tyre, the candour of dawn and the sapphires of the sky and the most beautiful ideas of human forms, as such excellent results cannot be produced by a human hand, if Heaven does not assist.

On the sides of the organ are figures in grisaille; on the pulpit the birth of Our Lord and other small stories; and beneath it near the tomb of Lorenzo Donato are two graceful youths in grisaille, with extinguished torches in their hands and skulls, and in the passage towards the sacristy there is a small painting of Saint Jerome.

Excited by such rare examples the Jesuit Fathers thought, in emulation of those at San Sebastiano, to make their church more distinguished and frequented, by embellishing their ceiling too, and they gave the task of painting it to Paolo.[28]

Now in the first painting, with the corners cut off, above the entrance, he depicted the embassy of the Angel to the Virgin announcing to her the birth of the Messiah, and at his sudden appearance she turns towards the divine messenger full of apprehension. The description of the appearance of that noble room embellished with arches supported on twisted columns covered in serpentine vines, the precious curtains, that surround the chaste bed, the various vestments of the celestial messenger, whose hems,

28. SS. Giovanni e Paolo, Venice

ruffled by the gentle wind form graceful swirls, the beauty of the wings painted with Iris's most beautiful colours, the divine resemblance, the tender action, the modest clothing, and finally the brilliance of the rays of the celestial spirit, it is not a task that can be encompassed by the pen of a mortal writer. The forms of the human speech are not equal to the task of expressing heavenly characters and deeds.

In the other painting towards the high altar are the shepherds around the crib, one of whom is sitting on an ox, which seems with its bellowing to revere in its own tongue the new-born Lord, and another is bringing in a further animal.

And in the oval placed in the centre the Virgin ascends to Heaven, lifted by angels adorned with various vestments bright with different colours, some she leans on, others perfume the ways of the sky with incense burners, and some pay court to the Celestial Queen by beating their golden wings. Around the sepulchre, where the holy body was laid at rest, are the apostles with their eyes fixed to Heaven, and holding books and lit torches, and others with clasped hands mourn the loss of Mary. A noble balustrade surrounds the sepulchre with a staircase in the middle which, even though it is not accurate at points, because of the placement of the figures, results in a pleasant view and produces a marvellous effect.

In smaller spaces on the sides are compartments with small narratives in green and red, of Moses, of Jonah, with others of the Old and New Testaments; but the marvellous painting of the Annunciation in that Order remains in the nuns' choir, who were installed there in the place of the said Fathers by the Senate; and in the tabernacle is the figure of the Redeemer.

It was not only Paolo's name that benefited because of what he had made, but also his fortunes, as he placed in the banks six thousand scudi, which in a few years he had collected thanks to his paint brushes, and these happily increased, because wealth accumulated through virtue has safe roots, and there is no worm of conscience to devour them. At this time Paolo went to Rome with Girolamo Grimani, Procurator of Saint Mark's, who had been appointed orator to the Pope, as his servant, not according to common custom to see the greatness of the court, but as a painter to witness the magnificence of the buildings, the paintings by Raphael, the sculptures of Michelangelo and in particular the celebrated statues, precious relics of Roman grandeur, about which he made observations, admiring that excellent form, which has always been followed and esteemed by the experts, and the beauty of the images of heroes, from which he took new ideas, as he then demonstrated in the works which we are going to describe, because the rare things that he saw and observed grew more refined and acquired degrees of higher perfection in his mind.

Having returned to Venice, great part of the paintings in the Council of Ten were given to him,[29] others to Zelotti, and those two spaces which contain Mercury and Peace, and Neptune with the trident on a sea horse are by the hand of a gentleman called Bazzacco, a good friend of Paolo, who was entrusted with the whole work.

Now in the main oval he painted Jupiter blasting Rebellion, Forgery, infamous Vice and Treachery, which errors are with great severity punished by the authority of this most serious Magistracy, and, all entangled together, fall to their ruin, terrified by Jupiter's thunderbolt; and among them is an angel with the decrees of that Council, who whips the air with its crisp hair and wings, which look as if they were made out of real feathers.[30] In his Jupiter the

29. Still in situ 30. Central canvas in the Musée du Louvre, Paris, the rest still in situ.

painter happily quoted the famous statue of Laocöon in the Belvedere in Rome, and in another figure the head commonly said to be of the Alexander, or as others say, of one of the Amazons and other casts which he kept in his studio.

Above the tribune he depicted a noble matron with broken shackles and chains in her hands, to signify the authority of that same Magistracy in dispensing mercy and punishment, looking upwards to a Heaven filled with Gods, indicating that Heaven will protect just princes.

In another compartment he painted Venice who receives from the hands of Juno jewels, crowns, and the doge's cap as a sign of the supreme honour, an ornament used in antiquity by the Trojans (from whom the Venetian people descend), as can be seen in the figure of Ganymede hanging in the middle of the Statuario della Repubblica, and as Virgil says through Romulus's mouth to the Trojans in these verses:

> Desidiæ cordi, iuvat indulgere choreis,
> Et tunicæ manicas & habent redimicula Mitræ.*

*In sloth you glory, and in dances join./Your vests have sweeping sleeves; with female pride/ Your turbants underneath your chins are tied. Virgil, *Æneid,* Book 9, translated by John Dryden

*Opposite: Venice and Juno, ca. 1555*

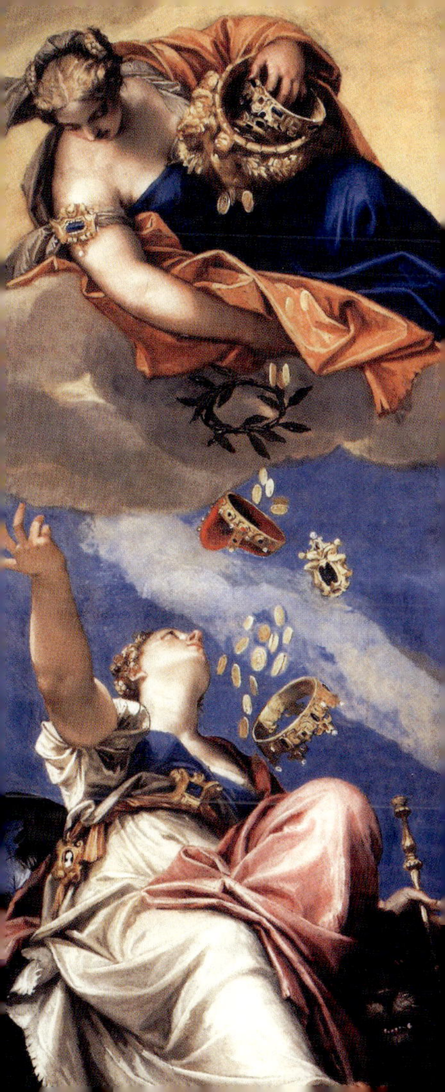

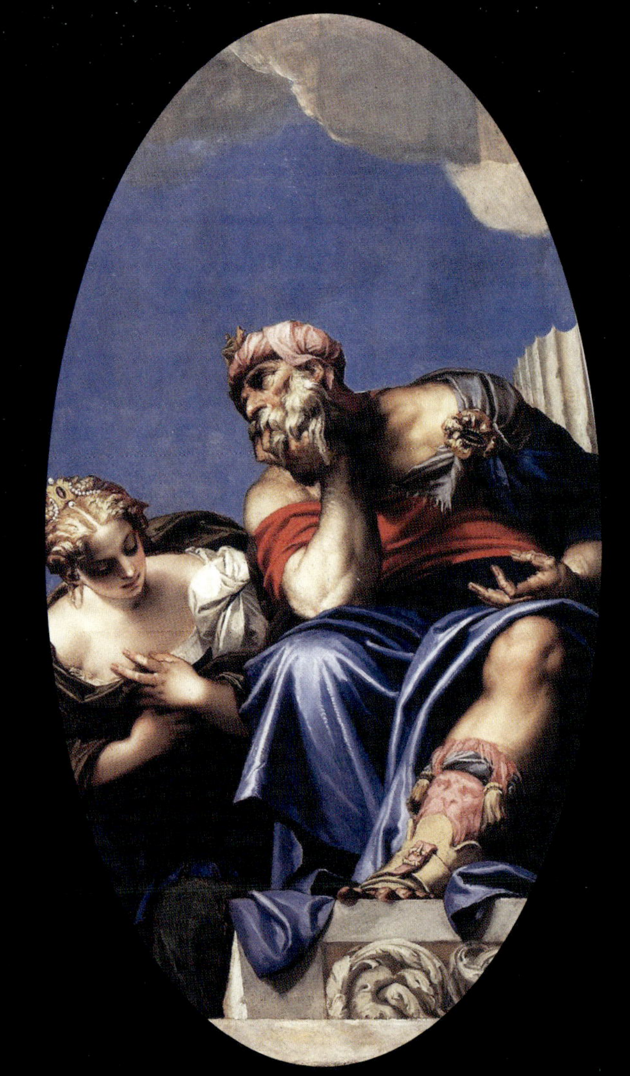

Which figure is of graceful magnificence in the alabaster of her neck and bosom.

In another smaller oval in the corner he painted a beautiful girl with rich ornaments in her hair, with her hands on her breast, looking downwards with great modesty, and an old man with a turban on his head and in barbarian guise, resting his chin on his right arm, with his white beard falling around it between his fingers, who represent the different conditions of people who appeal to that tribunal against oppression; and these two figures in particular, even though the others are all considered marvellous, are considered by other painters to be amongst the most exceptional that he painted, and Jacopo Palma used to say that in this case Paolo achieved the acme of delightfulness, and that in these he combined what was most erudite in the practice of antiquity and his own most noble style. Thus it happens that sometimes the painter, moved by an inspiration, attains the most sublime height of perfection, which he only rarely reaches. Again he arranged around the main oval four figures in grisaille pertinent to Dominion, and other beautiful naked figures.

Then in the year 1565, to complete the main

*Opposite: Youth and Old Age, ca. 1555*

chapel of San Sebastiano he painted the two large side canvases, in which he condensed the wonders and the marvels of art.[31]

One depicts Saints Marcellinus and Mark condemned to death if they did not renounce their faith in Christ within a certain time, and who in walking down the staircase of the palace of the prefect Cromatio, as they are taken by the henchmen to the prisons, are met by their father Tranquillus, held up by servants, who with poignant gestures beseeches them to avoid death, and to remain alive as a relief to his decrepit age, while their mother, enraged, follows them to restrain them, with her loose hair in the manner of a bacchant.

At the foot of the staircase are their wives, kneeling, showing them their young children, so that moved in their depths by paternal affection they will change their saintly intentions, and an imploring girl attaches herself to them with a childish gesture, but the generous knight Sebastian next to them incites them to martyrdom, and acts as an obstacle to that force which has power in the human heart, pointing towards a most beautiful angel in Heaven with the book of life in his hands. On the steps there is a very

31. Still in situ

realistic beggar and others clinging to the columns, in the distance well-dressed matrons admiring the constancy of the saints, and also charming views of architecture.

Greek eloquence celebrated the painting by Timanthes, in which the assiduous painter because he had displayed all the effects of piety and pain in the figures of the haruspex Calchas, Ajax, Achilles and Menelaus, covered the face of the father, Agamemnon, with a dark veil, hiding in this way that pain, which he considered impossible to express with his brush. Here Paolo surpassed him, as he not only depicted the feelings of piety and commiseration in the faces of the mother, the wives and the friends of the saints, but also he managed to express the nature of incomparable pain in the features of the sorrowful father.

In the other painting he represented Saint Sebastian tied to a wooden contraption ready for his martyrdom, with priests who try to persuade him to worship idols and so change the agony to delight and enjoy the flower of his youth, with noble characters, knights and others dressed in sumptuous manner, who admire his courage; and he portrayed Father Andrea (mentioned above) next to a column, and henchmen armed with sticks, servants holding dogs, and other decorations. The action is set underneath a portico supported by Corinthian columns, which adds much dignity to the invention.

He also painted there two altarpieces for smaller chapels, one with the Saviour at the river Jordan, the other with the Crucifixion with the Virgin Mary unconscious in the arms of her sisters, and the Magdalene with her arms wide open, who stares at her Lord hanging there, and lets fall liquid pearls from the springs of her eyes.[32] And from a beam in a chapel hangs a small picture with our Lady and a female virgin saint who offers a dove to the child, and in it there is the portrait of Father Michele Spaventi, Venetian.[33]

Finally he also gave the same Fathers a small banner for processions, with Saint Sebastian, thanks to which his merit was first known in Venice.

But the work which mainly brought greatness to Paolo's name were four large canvases of feasts painted by him at different times in that city, in which with diverse inventions he represented the sumptuous apparatus of regal banquets.

The first which he painted was the one for the

32. Still in situ 33. In the Grimani Chapel in San Sebastiano, Venice

*Opposite: The Baptism of Christ, ca. 1560 (Redentore, Venice)*

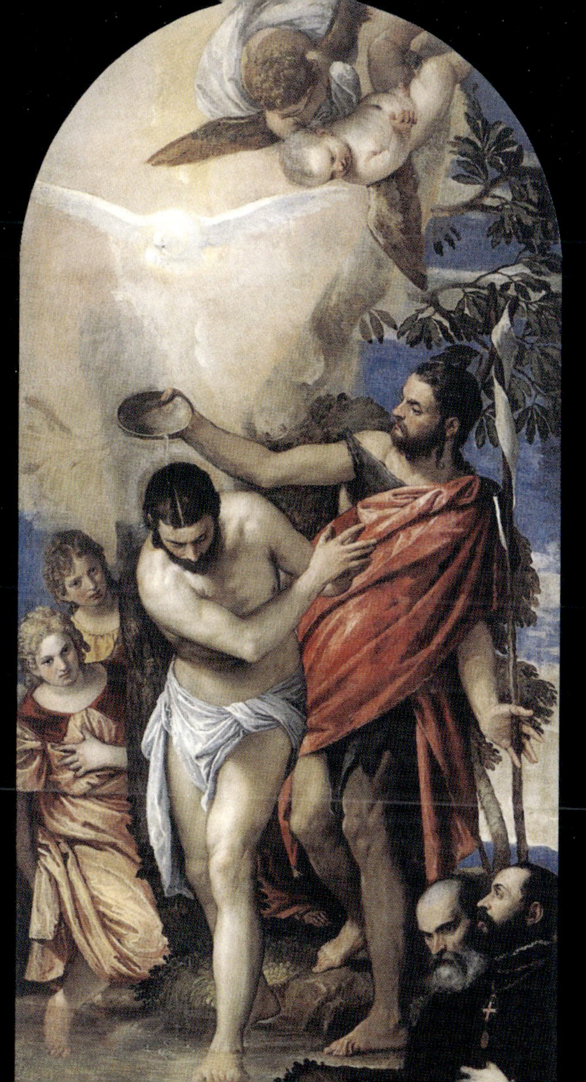

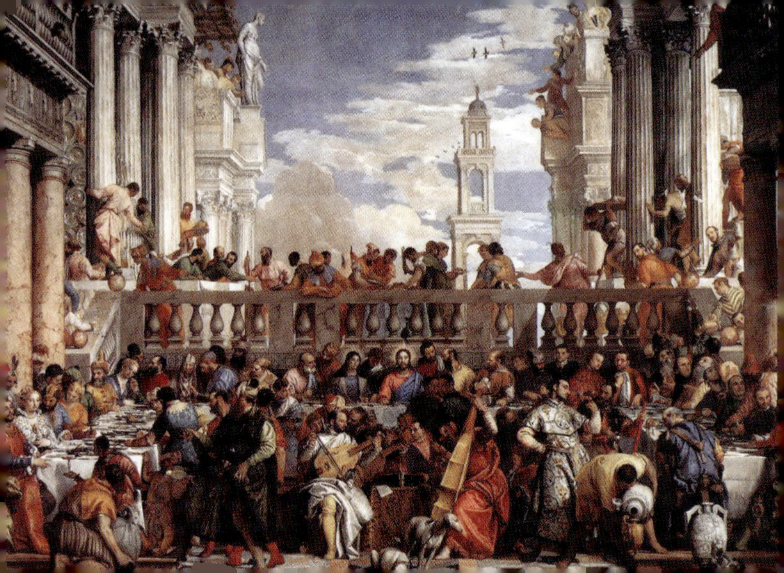

refectory of San Giorgio Maggiore, about twenty *braccia* wide, representing the wedding feast at Cana in Galilee, in which there are more than a hundred and twenty figures.[34]

The table is shaped like a U and is set up with silver and gold-fringed tablecloth arranged with delicacies, pies, fruit and appetising curiosities of every type. Christ sits in the middle, His mother to His side begging Him to take care for the missing wine. Beyond them on each side stand the apostles and a great number of guests dressed in rich clothes, and among them the portraits of many of those Fathers; which because Paolo was obliged to follow nature do not match the rest of the Ideas born from the imagination.

At one of the heads of the table sits the groom, resplendent in a coat and crimson and gold clothes, and the beautiful and happy bride next to him, in whose face the Graces breathe, and Loves sparkle; to them a black boy brings a glass of the water transformed into wine, while servants pour it from urns into smaller vases.

And not to scant any royal grandeur, the painter represented in the middle a choir of musicians who

34. Musée du Louvre, Paris

play violas, flutes, lutes and lyres, and sing from books. Behind the table is a great balcony, on which passing stewards prepare the food; and from the near-by staircases others bring some of it to the guests; and on the sides he placed two sets of columns and in the further distance a row of noble palaces stretches out in the distance with delightful art, from which many figures admire the sumptuous banquet.

The second banquet was the one for San Sebastiano, executed in the year 1570; and it is the supper of Simon, next to whom is a noble matron, with many guests present, servants with food, and there are perspectives with statues, most realistic dogs and other curiosities, and Judas standing from his chair looks with his surly eyes towards the Magdalene at the Saviour's feet, who having poured the precious liquid on them, is drying them with her hair.[35]

The third is in Santi Giovanni e Paolo, painted by him in the year 1573, and it is the one in the house of the moneylender Levi recounted by Saint Luke, which replaced the Last Supper by Titian which was burned; Frà Andrea de' Buoni, eager to see the painting renewed, offered Paolo a certain amount of money for this work, which he had left over from

35. Pinacoteca di Brera, Milan

charity and confessions, a price which, incidentally, a gentleman would not accept today to paint such a large canvas. But as the poor friar could not spend more, Paolo, forced by his pleas, wanted to satisfy him by accepting such an important commission, driven more by his wish for glory than by anything useful to him.[36]

The table is set under a spacious loggia, divided by three great arches, beyond which are beautiful structures of palaces, which make for a delightful view. In the middle is the Saviour, in front of him Levi dressed in crimson, and with him are many publicans sitting, and others interspersed with the apostles, where he depicted astonishing heads that make a singular effect, and he portrayed there the above mentioned Friar Andrea at the side with a napkin on his shoulder, and that figure alone would be worth all that was spent on the painting; and amongst the admirable things is the figure of the landlord leaning on a pedestal, and apart from the quality of this figure, his flesh is so fresh that he seems alive, and next to him is an Ethiopian servant with a Moorish outfit holding a basket, who seems to laugh and make those who look at him laugh.

36. Accademia, Venice

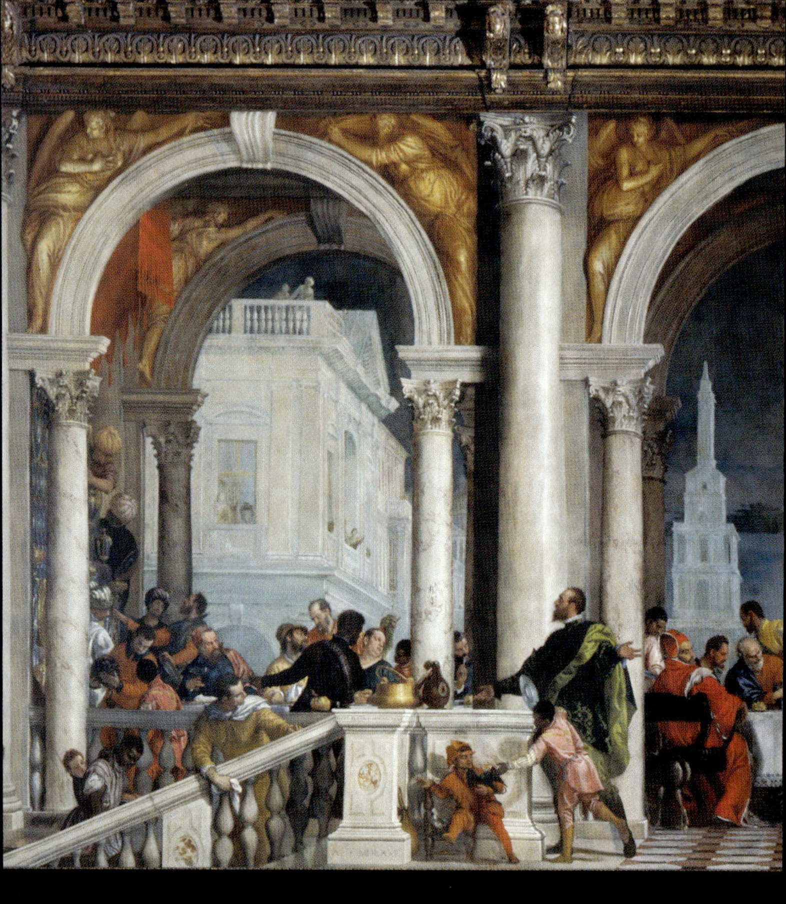

*The Feast in the House of Levi, 1573*

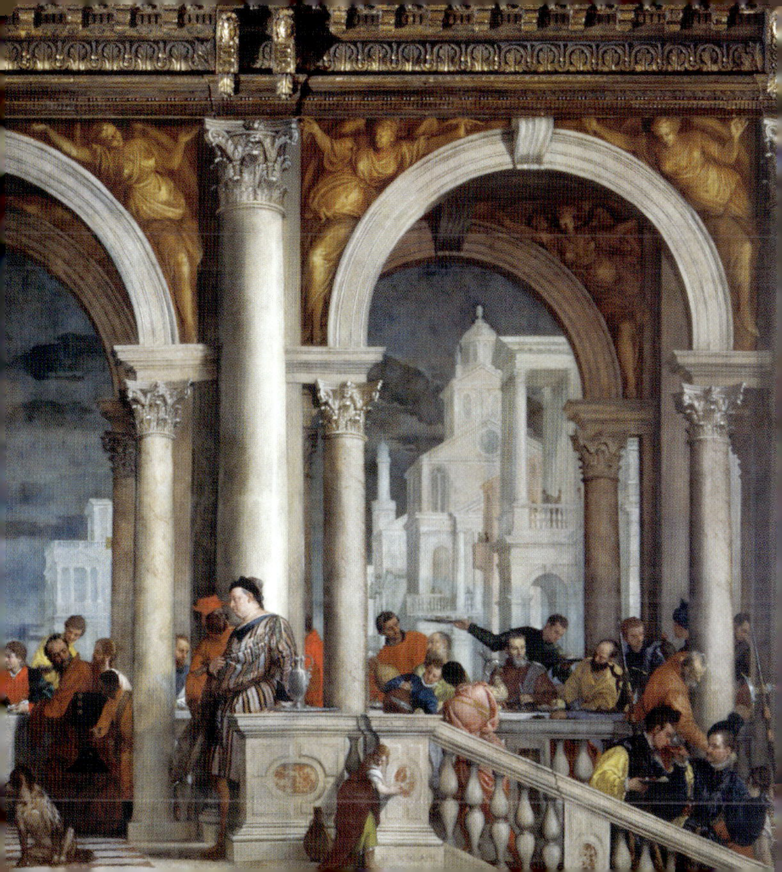

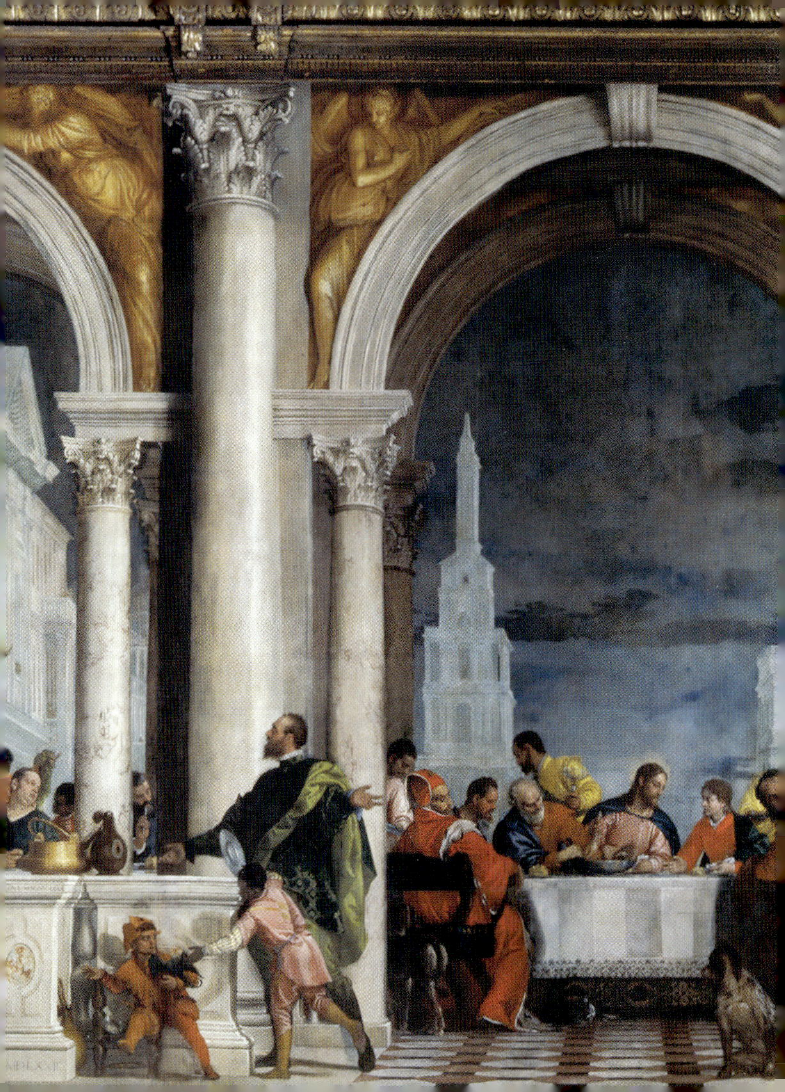

In sum, the whole work is handled with great mastery, as much as can be done in this genre, as Paolo did not want to reproach his conscience about it nor did he want to give Friar Andrea any reason to regret having badly spent his money.

The fourth is in the refectory of the Servite Fathers and in it he represented again the supper of Simon the leper with Christ, and the Magdalene is there in a different pose, penitent at his feet flooding them with her tears, and drying them with her hair which looks like gold.[37] Most precious tears, prized pearls, that liquefied in the alembic of the heart with the fire of ardent affection, you had the virtue of washing out the stains of a life of error. The table is set in the middle of a majestic theatre, around which are many columns, and in the centre are two flying angels with a short inscription: *Gaudium in cœlo super uno peccatore pœnitentiam agente*;* and here he also depicted Judas standing apart from the table in the act of reproaching the pious action of the penitent woman, and a number of characters sitting at the

* Joy shall be in heaven over one sinner that repenteth. Luke, 15, 7

37. Musée National du Château, Versailles

*Opposite: detail from The Feast in the House of Levi, 1573*

banquet, in which he portrayed many of the Fathers, who contributed some gift to the painter.

On the sides are two rich sideboards, from which servants take vases and plates in gold and silver; and in this according to the painters Paolo improved in style from the ones we have described, and in particular the figure of the Saviour looks unquestionably divine.

Even the royal banquets of Ahasuerus, of Cleopatra, of Alexander and of the Emperors, famous for the quality of the guests, for the quantity of golden vases sculpted by learned artists, for the precious foods, will concede the palm to such noble settings, because they could not achieve the grandeur of these ones painted by Paolo, commendable for the decorations, for the number of servants, for the divine characters, none of which can be described with words, as it is only his brush that can depict these things in a worthy manner.

The works, which he subsequently painted, were many. Amongst them is a great canvas for the church of San Silvestro, in which he painted the Adoration of the Magi, representing in a marvellous way the seated Virgin under a rustic hut built with many pieces of wood in the manner of a large edifice. From behind

*Opposite: The Adoration of the Magi, 1573*

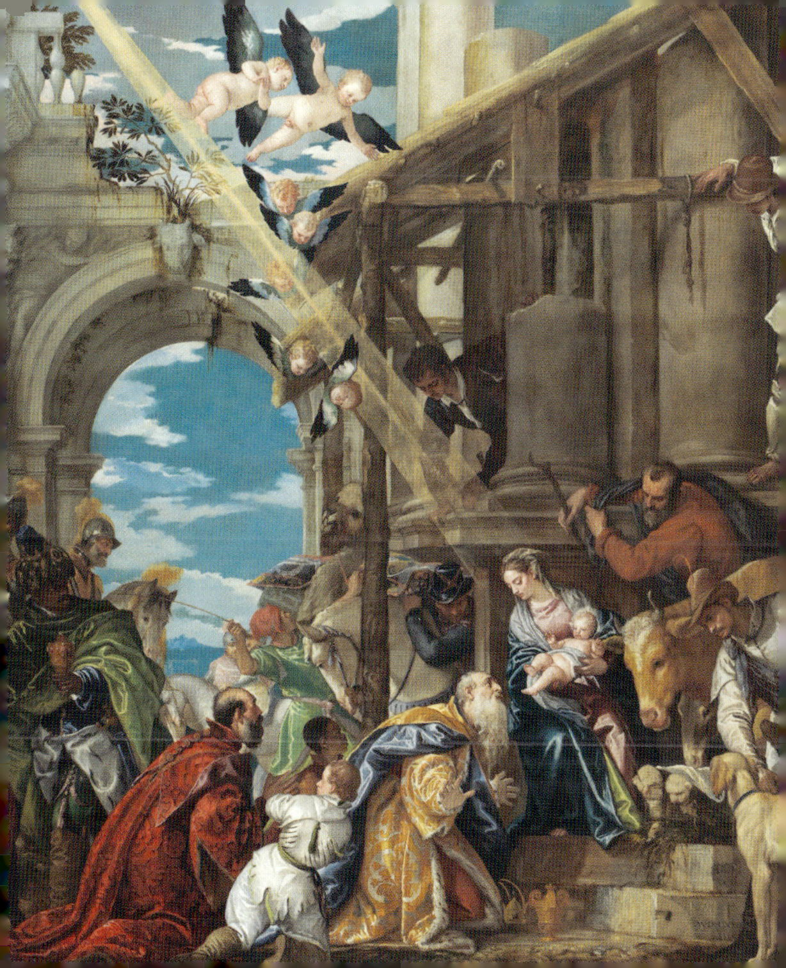

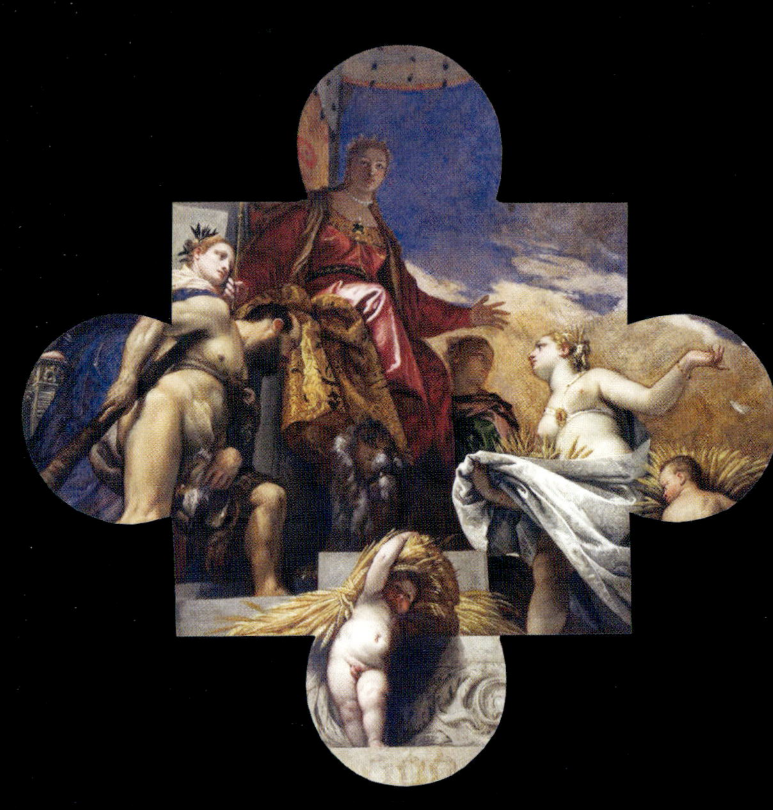

*Venice, Ceres and Hercules, ca. 1575*

an arch appear knights and servants, who direct camels loaded with goods, while their kings, prostrate, worship the newborn Jesus and Mary, from whose most pure face comes such splendour, that that rustic abode could well compete in magnificence with the palaces of the greatest monarchs.[38]

For the ceiling of the Magistrature of Wheat he painted the figure of Ceres, bringing to Venice crops of cereal, to signify the abundance of wheat, in which the Venetian state is rich, and the provision of the public; at her side is Hercules, leaning on his club, representing Heroic Virtue;[39] in the ceiling of the Magistrature of Wood he painted Venice, Neptune in front of her with tritons, who offer her gifts from the sea;[40] and in the office of the said magistrates he depicted the same in front of the Virgin.

At the same time in his youth he painted many things for other places, since his name had become universally known, and therefore foreign people competed in adorning their own countries with paintings by such a worthy hand.

He painted for the cathedral of Montagnana the altarpiece for the main chapel of the transfigured

38. National Gallery, London 39. Accademia, Venice
40. Szèpmüveszeti Muzeum, Budapest

Christ on Mount Tabor between Moses and Elijah surrounded by bright splendours, wanting in that way to show a token of celestial felicity to those closest to him, which cannot be achieved, except through suffering, after they had been talking amongst themselves of torments and death.[41] The disciples are on top of the mountain, one of them holding his hand in front of him to protect himself from the light, another one taking refuge under his cloak. And for the church dedicated to the Virgin in Lendinara he painted the Ascension of the Saviour.[42]

He sent another painting to the Fathers of the church of the Maddalena in Treviso, who were close to him, of Christ and the Magdalene in the garden, in which figure, it is said, he portrayed his wife, and next to her is her sister Marta and a portrait, and in the distance are angels guarding the sepulchre.[43]

Now while she is with her Lord, opening to him the feelings in her heart, we can see on another altar the Crucifixion, the fainting Mother, and the same Magdalene crying, and in a small processional banner the same penitent saint. And in truth those Fathers were fortunate because they managed to decorate their churches with the work of such a painter.

41. Still in situ 42. Still in situ 43. Still in situ

For the church of Sant'Agostino he painted the altarpiece of Saints Joachim and Anna, and Saints James and George standing, and for the refectory of the nuns of San Tommaso the marriage feast at Cana in Galilee,[44] and a painting of the dead Saviour which he gave to the abbess as a gift.

In Villa di Gravigna near Treviso there is one of his altarpieces with the portrait of the parish priest. In another in Casola in the house of the Cappello family is Saint Catherine with the wheel; and in the ceiling of a room the story of Danaë.

In the village of Sant'Andrea he painted in fresco Our Lady on a capital; in Rovere near Treviso he painted the picture with Saint Anthony praying and Saint Francis, receiving the stigmata, with the portrait of the head of the Ongarina family; and for the Compagnia della Croce of Cividale the figure of Saint Lucy.[45]

But let us turn towards Padua, and see in the grand church of the Benedictine Fathers the large canvas with the Martyrdom of Saint Justina, who fearlessly receives the wound in her breast from the executioner; the action of a magnanimous and regal

44. Palazzo di Montecitorio, Rome. In fact made for the refectory of the nuns at San Teonisto in Treviso. 45. National Gallery of Art, Washington

maiden, who, despite her tender years and her elevated state, offers herself in sacrifice to God. Small angels fly around the Heavens, who bring her palms and golden crowns, and above is the Saviour witnessing the scene surrounded by the angelic hierarchies, the Virgin and Saint John praying.[46]

Yet this painting is difficult to enjoy, being badly lit, and covered by the most over the top decoration; so its beauty is greatly compromised, because modern supervisors don't think of anything else but to amass piles of wood and mountains of stone instead of ornaments; and painting does not need anything but a small frame to surround it. In the rooms of the abbot there is a model for it which is changed in some parts;[47] and above the door of the sacristy the assumption of Our Lady.

On the altar of Andrea Capodivacca in the church of the Discalced Friars Minor there was an Ascension of Christ, but the bottom half of that canvas was cut out by a covetous hand, and only the Saviour remained because, as he was on his way up in the air, he was not reached by the knife; and Pietro Damino da Castelfranco painted the apostles again, and those Fathers wanted that this inscription should be recorded:

46. Still in situ   47. Musei Civici, Padua

Quod furto nefario elaboratissimæ tabulæ eximij Pauli
Veronensis ademptum fuerant, curantibus Cœnobij
Patribus & felici pennicillo
Petri Damini Castrofrancani suppletum est.
Anno Domini MDCXXV Die XXVIII Martij.*

In San Giovanni di Malta, known as 'of the boats', is the altarpiece of the Baptism of Christ,[48] and in the Maddalena another small painting with the Virgin and Child and a little angel who is hiding under her cloak, Saint Joseph, and the young Saint John the Baptist, a most precious painting.[49]

There were also in that city in the house of the Contarini family eight paintings of sacred scenes with almost life-size figures, in one of them was Our Lady with several saints; in another Christ amongst the Doctors;[50] the Centurion in front of the Saviour,

* What had been cut away by nefarious theft from the highly wrought painting of the excellent Paolo Veronese has been restored through the care of the Fathers of the Monastery and by the felicitous pencil of Pietro Damino of Castelfranco. The year of Our Lord 1625, the 28th day of March.

48. Palazzo Pitti, Florence  49. Carmini, Venice
50. Museo del Prado, Madrid

*Overleaf: Christ and the Centurion, ca. 1570*

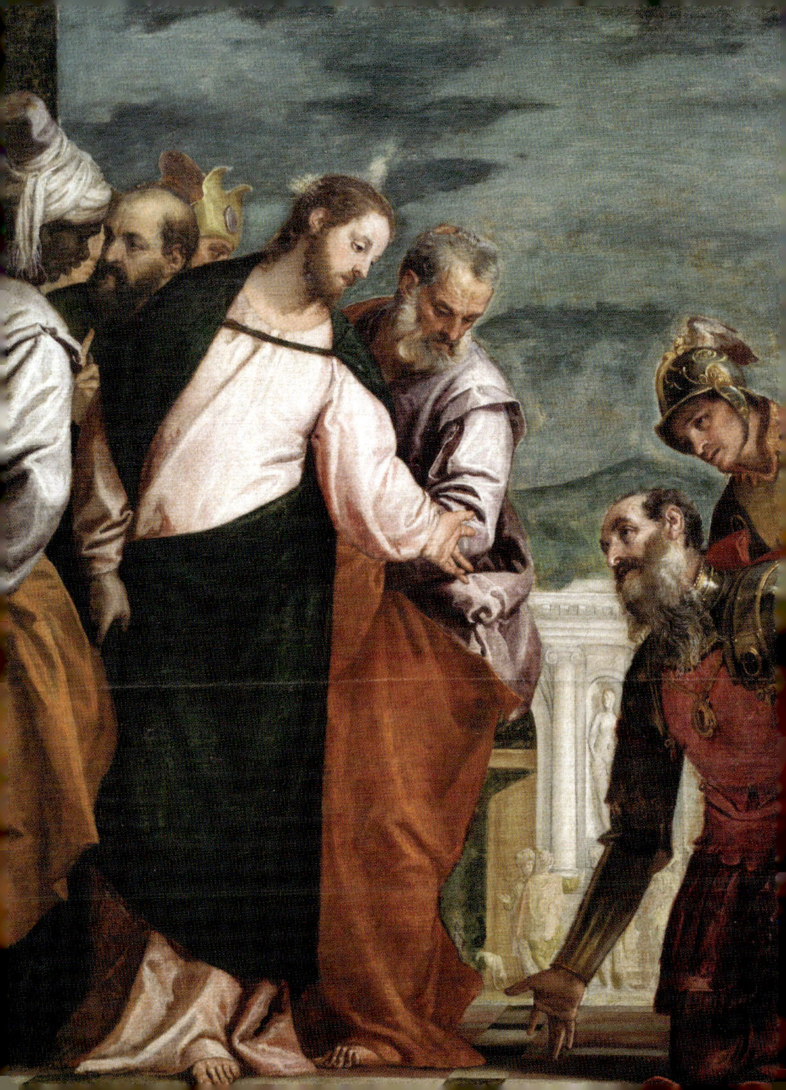

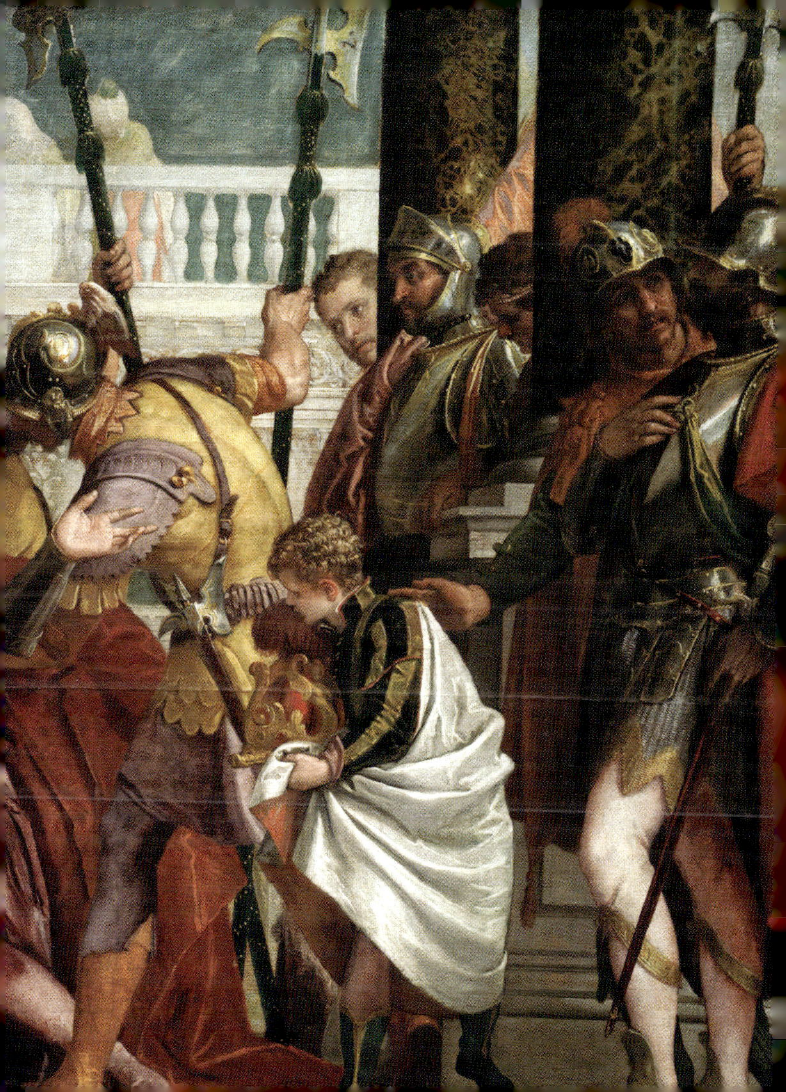

accompanied by servants, who guard his horse and his gilded helmet;[51] a scene of Saint Helena, who while sleeping dreams of a vision of the Cross held by two angels, that saintly queen nursing such a saintly thought in her mind, even though she was resting.[52] Often things that we conceive in our mind have been brought to us by ghosts to our intellect in our sleep. And there are the Four Seasons as figures. In the house of the Grimani family at the Prato della Valle there are two other history paintings, the Centurion,[53] and Moses as a child found in the river, a pretty composition.[54]

And continuing our journey to Vicenza, we can admire on the altar of the Cogoli family in Santa Corona the Magi who having arrived in Bethlehem are worshipping the Messiah, and there is an interweaving of coarse wood over a building in ruins, through which are small angels flying, in the middle of whom sits the Virgin, whose beauty and good looks are without any doubt beyond our understanding; and the majesty of those kings surpasses any earthly magnificence; in the same way the two pages

51. Museo del Prado, Madrid 52. National Gallery, London
53. Gemaldëgalerie, Dresden 54. Gemaldëgalerie, Dresden

*Opposite: St Helena, ca. 1570*

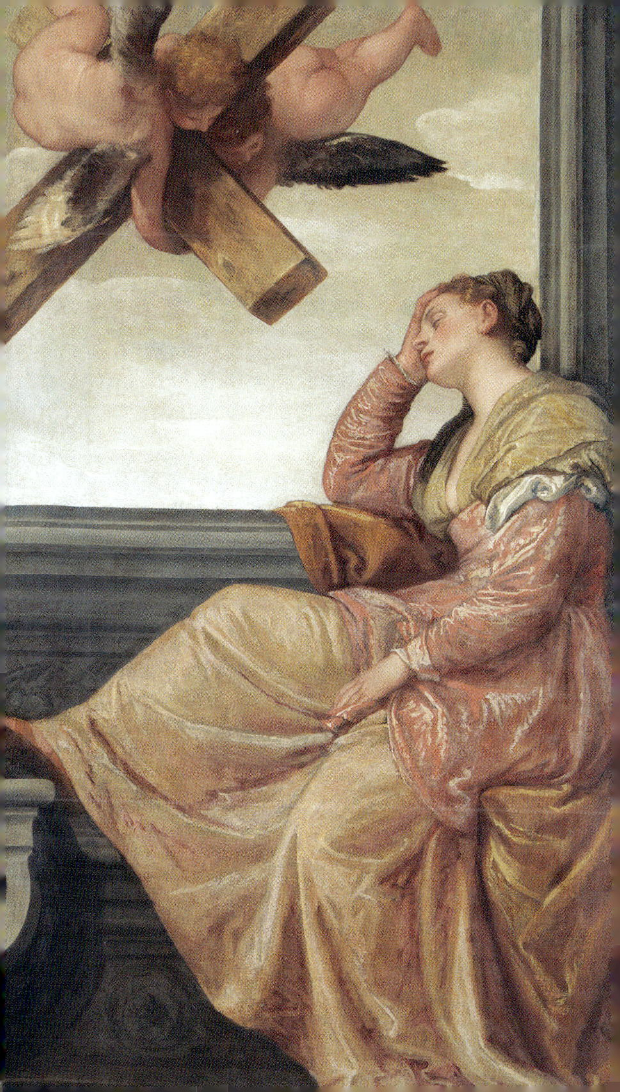

who are serving the first king are remarkable; and it is curious to see that a mule, emerging from one side, is carrying the arms of the donors in the middle of the harness, with which it is blindfolded.[55]

Then for the Fathers of the Madonna del Monte, so named after the hill which overlooks the city, surrounded on every side by pleasant mountains, where Vertumnus and Bacchus vie in the abundance of the finest fruit and grapes, he painted for their refectory the meal that Saint Gregory the Great gave for the poor, where Christ having become his guest sits with him at the table, to demonstrate, how grateful he was to the saintly Pope for his piety.[56] There are many pilgrims around depicted with the noblest faces, as Paolo did not know how to represent his figures if not always in a noble manner. Two cardinals with crimson robes sit in front, one of whom is looking through a large monocle, where the painter depicted a certain habit of the character, which in truth is praiseworthy. He ingeniously placed the prior beside a column, who stands out wonderfully for the black of his robes; and arranged on stairs on either side are the servants, who dispense the leftovers of the papal table to other needy people.

55. Still in situ 56. Still in situ

But the beauty of such rare objects should not delay us from seeing the works in Verona. In the church of San Giorgio Paolo painted for the high altar the saintly knight on his knees, stripped by henchmen, persuaded by priests to offer incense to the idol of Apollo; his face reveals an unvanquished soul, unafraid of the tyrant's threats, strengthened by seeing the Virgin flanked by the Theological Virtues in the sky.[57]

Below the organ is Saint Barnabas Apostle, shown in the centre of a tribune, who is healing an invalid while reading the Gospels over him, and men and women holding torches look on and pray; while others bring invalids to the saint, for him to cure them.[58]

And even though Paolo conducted himself in an exceptional way with his first altarpiece, nonetheless other painters believe than in this second one he improved in a certain way his manner; and that narrative could not be represented with more piety or devotion. In such worthy paintings Paolo demonstrated his affection towards his homeland, that had esteemed him so little. And in the sacristy of the Fathers of the Vittoria there is a small painting of the Saviour taken down from the cross, lying on his

57. Still in situ 58. Musée des Beaux-Arts, Rouen

mother's lap, with the Maries crying.[59] In San Paolo there is another altarpiece with Our Lady on a plinth, the Baptist, and the parish priest portrayed from life.[60]

But here let us further add the works by his hand that are in private collections in that city. In the houses of the Marquises della Torre I saw a painting of the child Moses found in a reed basket in the river by the daughter of Pharaoh,[61] and a mythological scene in another small canvas in the houses of Counts Giusti; a naked Venus looking at herself in the mirror[62] and the portrait of a matron with a little girl next to her with the Bevilacqua family.[63] In the rooms of the Abbot of San Nazaro there was a Nativity of Christ, which was given by those Fathers to Cardinal Ludovisi. It is now in Rome in the collection of Prince Ludovisi. Doctor Curtoni has a Saviour held up by two angels, the story of Actæon, with many naked Nymphs, and a Europa; a drawing in grisaille of Virtue, who runs away from an ugly snake, which stands for Vice.[64]

59. Museo di Castelvecchio, Verona 60. Still in situ
61. Museo del Prado, Madrid 62. Joslyn Museum, Omaha
63. Musée du Louvre, Paris 64. Ecole des Beaux-Arts, Paris

*Opposite: The Finding of Moses, ca. 1575-80*

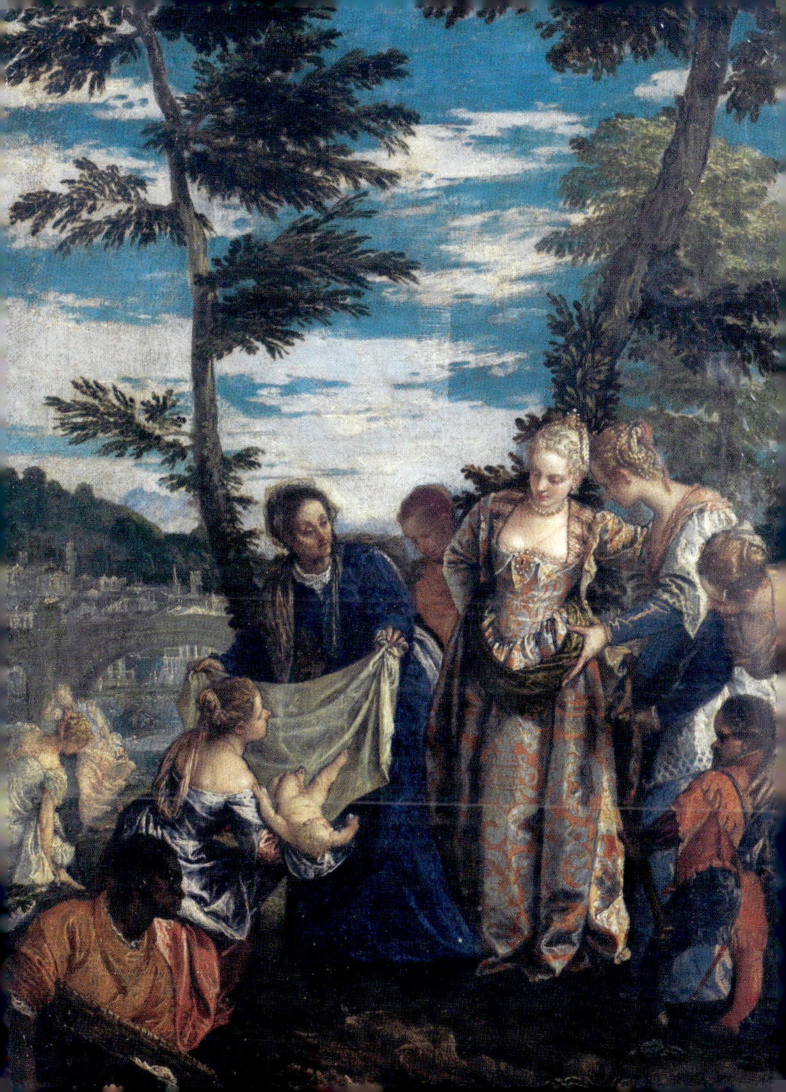

In the study of Cristoforo and Francesco Muselli, who share the love of their beloved dead father towards Painting, are the following paintings by this hand. A Virgin with the child asleep in sweet slumber on her knees. The marriage of Saint Catherine with the child Jesus, who is reaching out from his mother's arms, and Joseph and the Baptist are there as witnesses, and a lovely lady portrayed from life. The Saviour at the river Jordan with the most beautiful angels, who hold his clothes. Christ at the table with the two disciples Luke and Cleophas in the act of blessing the bread, which breathes from every part the grace of Heaven. There are servants who bring food to the table, and a charming girl plays with a dog. Nor have I ever seen a work more gracious and beautiful. Another image of the Virgin Mary with Saint John, who plays with the child Jesus, and Saint Joseph resting in the shadow of joyful plants. Two exceptional inventions of Jacob at the well with Rachel; and Christ with the woman taken in adultery, who stands with downcast eyes, and blushes for her fault, while the accusing scribes insist that she should be punished.[65]

They also have a life-size Venus, to whom even the

65. Possibly the painting in the National Gallery, London.

hardest heart would consecrate his love as a perfect image of beauty, and Love is at her feet with his customary harness.

Besides these paintings I have described, those gentlemen also own some drawings on coloured paper with white lead highlights, of which it would be long to describe all the inventions; but we will only mention some haphazard thoughts, that he annotated with his own hand on the back of some of them, and which were sent for pleasure to those who had asked for them, and we will record them in the same order.

Fourth Painting. The ways and the postures in which the Virgin has been painted are infinite; and she was represented by Albrecht Dürer almost always in the same way, painted with her Child, always nude, in her arms. The Greeks always painted him wearing swaddling clothes, as they were not skilful in depicting bodies. Every figure of a child nonetheless can be painted nude just as well as dressed. Buonarroti depicted the sleeping Baby and the Mother, reading a book; nor did I ever see her next to the crib, dressing the Saviour. I would paint the Child in the crib with angels around him, holding baskets of fruit and flowers, and playing various instruments, and some of them singing to the sleeping

Baby, and the Virgin would hold Him close, together with Saint Anne.[66]

Fifth Painting. I painted once for my room a picture of Our Lady, seated with a book in front of her and with her eyes raised to Heaven, with her hand on her breast, and with her mother asleep on one side, and for the picture I devised many angels, one of whom held a phoenix, another a crown of thorns and one a crown of stars, the sun and the moon, covering the floor with fruit, flowers, olive and palm branches, to depict how all seasons and all things stand before the Creator, and how he is attended by the angels his ministers, and Mary taking part in the offerings and the divine mysteries.[67]

Sixth Painting. If I will ever have time, I would like to represent a magnificent banquet under a noble loggia, with the Virgin, the Saviour and Joseph, having them waited on by the richest cortège of angels that one can imagine, who will serve them regal food and an abundance of sumptuous fruits in silver and gold dishes. Others will be bringing precious provisions in transparent glasses and in gilded cups, to demonstrate the office provided by the blessed spirits to their God, as it will be explained better at the end of the book,

66 Musée du Louvre, Paris. 67 Private collection

for the knowledge of painters and the pleasure of the lovers of Virtue; of which invention I saw a most extraordinary drawing.[68]

In Brescia there is the altarpiece with Saint Afra in the church built in her name, who suffers her martyrdom on a catafalque; at the foot of which are the bodies of the martyred saints, and angels fly from the sky with palms and garlands; in which work Paolo proved himself not less worthy than Tintoretto or Bassano, who had painted other altarpieces in that church.[69]

In the houses of the Lanzi family in Bergamo, there is the figure of Christ, Ecce Homo, about which an extraordinary event is recounted by a man worthy of belief, that as the steward of that family was trying to exculpate himself of a certain accusation, and as the master did not believe him, he said that he would pray that image to give a sign over the life of his only son, who within a few days died, and this was said to be a miracle that God wanted to demonstrate through that figure painted by Paolo.

Finally in Genoa, to conclude the account of the foreign works, there is an altarpiece with the Crucifixion, the Virgin and Saint John.[70] It is said

68. Kunsthalle, Bremen 69. Still in situ 70. Palazzo Bianco, Genoa

that in the house of the Grimani there is the visit of the Magi, and the marriage of Saint Catherine martyr; subjects that that painter represented differently several times. There is the dead Saviour in the houses of Francesco Lomellini; and in those of Felice Pallavicini another two canvases of the flight of our Lady to Egypt and of Christ among the Doctors.

Now we will consider certain works in fresco, in addition to the ones mentioned above, which were painted by Paolo to please great lords, though it seems impossible that in the short span of his life he painted so many works. But this happened because of his facility for painting, as he never put his brush in the wrong place, and because his figures were always finished at the second brushstroke.

Overlooking the Grand Canal in the houses of the Cappello family he painted certain figures of Ceres, Pomona, Pallas and other gods. The ones above were painted by his friend Zelotti.[71]

In Murano in the palace of Camillo Trevisani, which is said to have been built following the designs of Monsignor Daniele Barbaro, who wrote on Vitruvius (and where in the past gentlemen and ladies would entertain themselves with parties), he

71. Destroyed

painted on the ceiling of a room on the ground floor the heavens inhabited by the gods with flying putti, one of which brings the royal diadem, the sceptre and jewels to Jupiter, as the fount of greatness; another brings the plectrum, above which is a crown of laurels, to Apollo; to Mars decorated armour, while a putto holds his sword; and nearby Cynthia holds the moon in her hand and has her dog by her; to Venus they bring a garland of roses, and she holds Cupid in her arms and has another child at her feet; to Saturn set-squares and the pendulum; to Mercury the cap, books and musical instruments, and winged sandals. Other putti hold mitres, lutes, guitars, and fly in beautiful postures; and the painting is surrounded by a noble frame painted to look like stucco, with satyrs and gilded heads on medallions so well painted that they seem in relief.[72]

In four compartments in the frieze he painted Music, Study, Astrology, and Fortune who pours gems over a drowsy man, and two figures in grisaille flanking the fireplace, who do not look painted until you touch them.[73]

72. The much damaged and detached frescoes are now in the Musée du Louvre, Paris. 73. What remains of the much damaged frescoes is still in situ.

The person who thinks that he can list the quantity of flowers, that bright Spring scatters out in the delightful gardens, or the great amount of fruit which is distributed with generous hand by fructiferous Autumn, will also be able to describe the outstanding qualities of such erudite and exceptional figures.

Poets can well illustrate at their will majestic Jupiter, Saturn serious and burdened with thoughts, dauntless Mars in whose face fury stands out, Mercury agile in walking around the paths of the air, Apollo with delicate features over whose head flutters a cloud of curly and blonde hair and with a blue sash with a golden knot hanging to his side holding the musical instrument; and Venus, finally, so beautiful that everywhere she breathes grace and love, and all the forms of speech will be defective compared to those that Paolo's brush was able to compose, and pens declare themselves defeated by his lines and colours, and inks blush.

In the rooms on the floor above he painted in the ceiling of a room Venus carried in the air by Cupids. Above one of the doors, that serves as an entrance, he painted Janus and Saturn; and Jupiter and Juno on each side. Bacchus and Apollo above another door, and on either side Neptune on the back of a sea-horse, and Cybeles sitting on lions; and at the top he painted some Cupids, two of whom pour a vase of water from the river Lethe over two torches, which has the virtue of extinguishing the flame of Love, and another two try to take a palm branch from each other's hands, to demonstrate with their rivalry that one is superior in loving to the other. And on the walls he arranged festoons of branches and fruits, landscapes, small scenes painted in yellow; and above the door to the nearby loggia he did other figures in grisaille, helmets, armours and small scenes from the history of Alexander in feigned bronze; in which works Paolo demonstrated the talent he had for any manner of painting.

For the contemplation of Francesco Erizzo he then painted also in fresco in the main hall of his palace at San Cassiano, now belonging to the Morosini family (built to the designs of Andrea Palladio), ancient buildings and landscapes; and he left there also by his hand a statue in stucco of Mars (the others were carved by Vittoria), in which one can observe his manner of painting.

On the façade towards the canal he depicted Neptune in triumph on a shell pulled by sea-horses and with tritons around him who hold lamps, flags and different weapons, and blow on twisting conch-shells; and putti fly in the sky holding bunches of arrows, quivers, turbans, spears and crowns in their hands, and Fame blows her golden trumpet. In between the windows he painted Minerva and Peace in grisaille, and at their feet the Seasons; Diana with her dog for Spring; Ceres with a cornucopia filled with fruit and wheat for Summer; Bacchus who squeezes a bunch of grapes in the mouth of a tiger for Autumn; and an old man wrapped in a hooded cloak for Winter; and as a decoration around the windows he painted human torsos, and over the door two slaves and other eccentricities painted with such delicacy that they could not be more softly coloured, demonstrating that they seem to have been produced there by nature.[74]

For Girolamo Grimani, Procurator of Saint Mark's, he further painted in fresco certain mythological scenes on the façade of his delightful palace at Oriago, and certain erudite figures on the frontispiece;[75] and at Villa di Magnadole in the houses of the Giunti family, now belonging to the Foscarini family, he painted in the sala scenes from Roman history in between architectural elements.[76]

Here we will briefly note other paintings in the churches of Venice, because the works that had to be

74. Destroyed 75. Destroyed 76. Destroyed

painted in that city were always shared with Paolo, seeing that his manner was universally appreciated.

In San Francesco della Vigna there are three altar-pieces. One in the chapel of the Giustiniani family with a seated Virgin at the top, Saint Joseph with her and the young Baptist holding the small lamb; at the bottom Saint Anthony Abbot and Saint Catherine, a delightful figure and highly esteemed;[77] the second in the chapel of the Badoer family with Christ rising from the tomb;[78] the former have been made known by the prints of Carracci, the latter by those of Kilian.

The third is in the sacristy with the same Virgin between two most joyful angels, who play lutes; and kneeling below are Saint John the Baptist and Saint Jerome, dressed as a cardinal, who reads a book held by a boy, a portrait from life of a member of the Cuccina family, owners of the altar, endowed by Giovanni and Girolamo Cuccina in the year 1562; which picture was repainted by Paolo on the wall, after the first perished in the fire of the Arsenal in 1574; but this one because of the humidity of the plaster, is deteriorating, as marble better survives the injuries of time. But it might happen that it will be better preserved in these pages.[79]

77. Still in situ 78. Still in situ 79. Destroyed

Eight further altarpieces are scattered through other churches in Venice, one of the Crucifixion in the Incurabili;[80] the second in San Giuliano with the dead Saviour on a cloud supported by angels, and at his feet Saints James, Mark and Jerome, painted for the Cavalier Vignola;[81] and in the chapel of the Sacrament there is the Last Supper.[82] The third is in San Giacomo dell'Orio in the chapel of Saint Lawrence, with three saints, and below, the Martyrdom of the deacon saint,[83] and over the benches of the choir he depicted the Theological Virtues in a tondo and the Doctors of the Church in the corners, which turned out to be one of his most charming and beautiful paintings.[84]

The fourth, in San Polo, shows of the marriage of Our Lady with Saint Joseph.[85] Two more are in San Pantaleon, in the one on the high altar is the saint dressed with a ducal cloak, who heals a youth held by the parish priest.[86] The other on the altar of the Lanaiuoli shows Saint Bernardino to whom the name of Jesus is brought by angels.[87] The seventh at

80. San Lazzaro dei Mendicanti, Venice 81. Still in situ
82. Still in situ 83. Still in situ. The predella is now lost.
84. Still in situ 85. Still in situ. In fact it represents Anna and Joachim. 86. Still in the church but on a different altar.
87. Still in situ

the nuns of Sant'Andrea, where in a rustic hut the Cardinal Saint is reading and beating his chest with a hard rock.[88] And finally the eighth was at the Servites with the Queen of Heaven over a pergola, Saint John and a bishop below, and this was stolen by a sacrilegious hand, and subsequently renewed by the excellent brush of Alessandro Varotari.[89]

In Santa Sofia he depicted the Supper of Maundy Thursday, and the table is rendered in perspective, with Christ our Lord at its head in the act of giving Holy Communion to the apostles, who prostrate themselves at his feet one by one.[90]

In San Geminiano following the same style he painted on the organ shutters two bishop saints, Saint John and the knight Saint Menna.[91]

But this is the time to talk about the paintings in the Doge's Palace, recounting things, as far as possible, in chronological order. As two rooms, the Election Hall and the Council Hall, which burned down in 1576, had to be redecorated, the Senate decreed that they should be renovated in the noblest form, and that they should be adorned with new paintings, delegating those improvements to Jacopo

88. Accademia, Venice 89. ie. Il Padovanino. Now in Accademia, Venice. 90. Pinacoteca di Brera, Milan 91. Galleria Estense, Modena

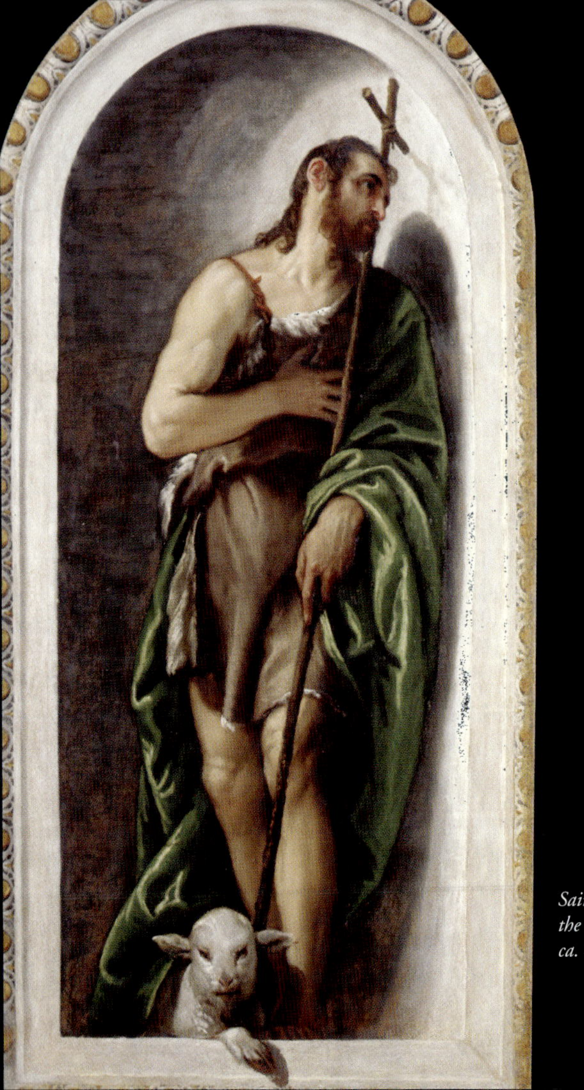

*Saint John the Baptist, ca. 1560*

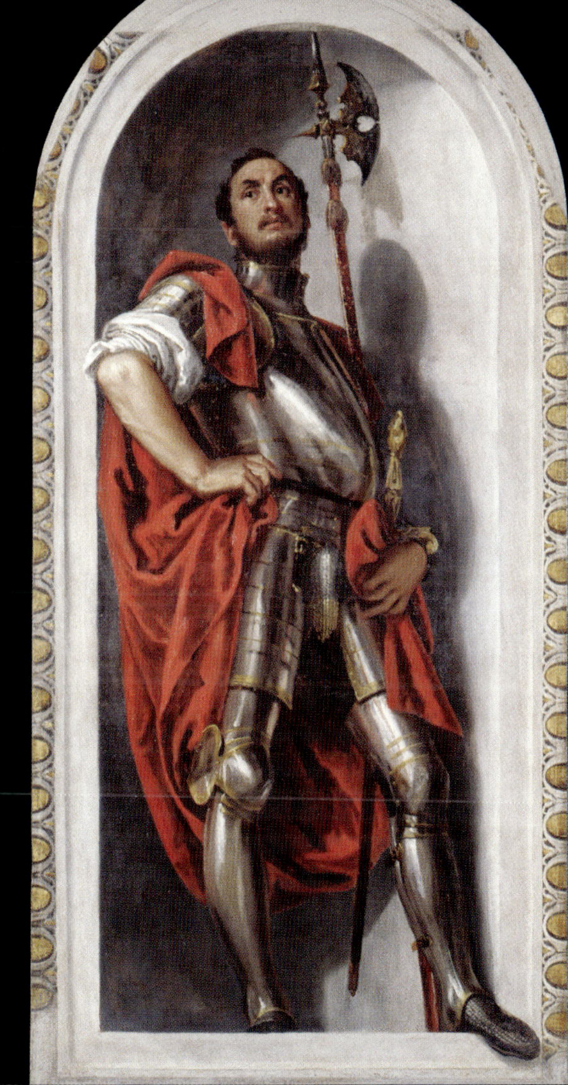

*Saint Menna,*
*ca. 1560*

Soranzo, knight and Procurator, Francesco Bernardo, Jacopo Marcello and Jacopo Contarini, who after careful consideration about the scenes which were to be painted for the dignity and majesty of the Republic (having heard the views of Don Girolamo Bardi, a Camaldolese monk who was an expert in narratives), agreed unanimously on the persons of Tintoretto and Paolo, to whom Palma, Bassano and others were later added because of the quantity of works that had to be painted.

Having been allotted the subjects, every one of the chosen artists confirmed with great readiness their part, only Paolo to everybody's great astonishment was never seen at the Magistracy. When on encountering Contarini, one of the Signori, he was bitterly reproached because although he was included as one of the main painters, he had not appeared like the others to claim his part, as if he did not greatly value the honour which had been bestowed on him or the public service. Paolo answered that he considered it his highest duty to be able to serve his prince every time he was required, but that it was not for him to look for new employments, of which he had plenty, and that this should not be ascribed to lack of the love he had, as a good citizen, for his homeland.

But, gently persuaded by Contarini, the next

morning he appeared at the Magistracy and the main oval over the tribune in the main hall was given to him, with a further picture on each side.[92] Now for this so worthy occasion, which was going to perpetuate his name in such a conspicuous place, Paolo gave birth to a precious demonstration of his merit. Over the clouds he depicted Venice between two towers, similar to ancient Rome, crowned by Victory with a regal diadem, as queen ruling over the Adriatic sea and the noblest cities of Lombardy, and watchful Fame, who blows her golden trumpet, publicising her glories. With her are Honour, Liberty with a cap of liberty on a pole, Peace, Juno with the sceptre and imperial crown in her hands, to signify her majesty, Ceres nude and crowned with ears of wheat and holding a cornucopia filled with sheaves, and Content, as she relishes such leisure and honours. Behind her a splendid façade rises supported by twisted columns and at the top of the cornice are two figures in feigned bronze, Mercury and Hercules, standing for eloquence and fortitude; and underneath it there is a balcony, where are people of different kinds, referring to the many nations which are subject to her, with noble matrons, carrying the most beautiful

92. Still in situ

young girls in their arms, looking at those gods in admiration. He equally arranged on that level knights, soldiers and prisoners, instruments of war, with many other bizarre things which make the composition animated and decorative. Here there is no lack of matter to praise Paolo's superhuman imagination and powers of invention, as he embellished every part of that work with such magnificence and beauty, but it suffices to say that he was born to show how the inhabitants of Heaven and earthly splendours look.

In one of the paintings he depicted the capture of Smyrna, when the general appointed for the task by the Republic was Pietro Mocenigo, working with the Papal Legate. In this attack the frightened Turks took refuge in hiding-places in their houses, and the Venetians carried off a rich haul of men, spoils, gold, silver and precious vases; and underneath the painting can be read:

> Ad cæteras vastationes direptionesque Asiaticas
> Classis Veneta Smyrnam expugnat.*

In the other he represented the defence of Scutari, achieved because of Antonio Loredan's bravery, which

*In addition to other devastations and depradations in Asia, the Venetian fleet conquers Smyrna.

happened in the following manner. As Suleiman and Ali Bey, Commanders of the Ottoman armies, were camping with their numerous army below Scutari, they stormed the city walls with the usual tumult of janissaries and archers; but the citizens together with the Venetian soldiers, fortified by Loredan, who performed the task of a courageous captain in inciting them to battle, reminding them of their devotion to the Republic, the love for their homeland, the honour of the Faith, the safety of their wives and children, and the hope of victory, fiercely slaughtered the Turks with stones and fire enclosed in terracotta pots, killing three thousand of them, so that the enemy was forced to retreat, as it is well expressed by the Author's brush, and underneath it is recorded:

> Scodra bellico omni apparatus diu vehementerque à Turcis oppugnata, acerrima propugnatione retinetur.§

It remains for us to mention some extraordinary paintings, to which Veronese brought the ultimate in grace and perfection, so that they appear as those imaginary beauties that sometimes are formed in the mind; and therefore the world judged that Art would

§ Scodra [Scutari], under intense and prolonged assault by a powerfully equipped Turkish force, is retained by a most vigorous defence.

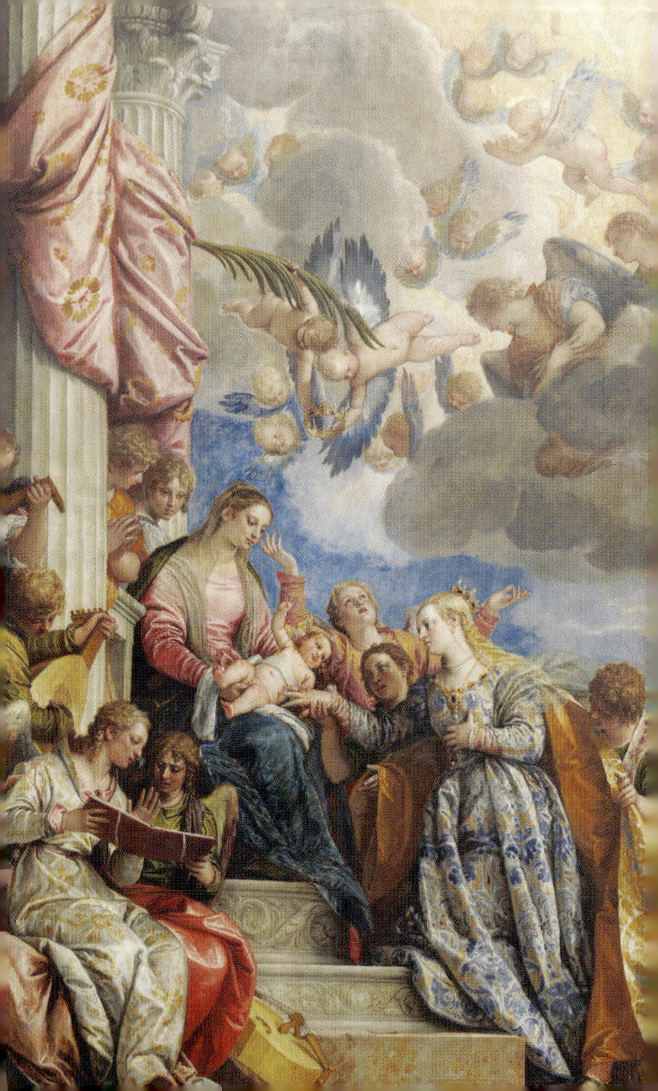

not be able to produces further great things.

For the nuns of Santa Caterina he painted on the high altar that saintly queen at the moment when, having become transfigured by her baptism, she was enraptured in a divine ecstasy and celebrated her wedding with the King of Heaven, who places on her finger a gold ring to signify eternal marriage.[93] Here, instead of courtiers, angels clad in precious vestments, embellished with the work and embroideries of the Arachnes of Heaven, attend the ceremony, and some of them play the sweetest symphonies with lutes and lyres to make the royal wedding happier. In that truly praiseworthy work there is no part which is not seasoned with precious forms of beauty and with most pleasant colouring; so the eye enraptured by such delightful objects, enjoys a display of celestial beatitude, extraordinary grace that had been given to Paolo's brush.

Here we recount again how he painted for certain nuns a painting of Paradise in standard size, in which following the good rules of art he represented the most distant figures less finished and made subdued in colour, giving the advantage in strength and beauty to

93. Accademia, Venice

*Opposite: The Mystic Marriage of Saint Catherine, ca. 1565-70*

the nearer ones; but as the figures did not appear beautiful in the eyes of the nuns, because blues, greens and vermilions did not highlight his talent, and as they could not distinguish the threads of hair or the eyelids, they were dissatisfied. When a certain Flemish painter came by the monastery with his tiny pictures illuminated with gold and bright colours, which made the eyes of those nuns fall in love with them in a manner in which they blamed their luck for not having found this kind of painter for the picture of Paradise; and as they ripped those small paintings from each other's hands, looking at them in a womanly fashion; see sister, one of them would say, how well depicted these eyes are and how beautiful this blonde hair is? Another would praise the coral-red lips, and some the subtlety of colouring, every one of them calling upon them a thousand blessings as if in competition. Therefore the foreign artist having become aware of their little understanding, offered to transform Paolo's work in one by his hand for the price of his expenses, promising colours from Heaven's mines; the nuns considering the proposal advantageous, exchange the gem for crystal, and afterwards the cunning painter having taken the painting somewhere else, sold it (even though its author was still alive) for four hundred scudi.

With similar skills Paolo painted another five altarpieces. In Ognissanti on the high altar that Glory of the Blessed, where at the top is the Virgin crowned by God the Father and the Son, and, above, on the clouds in several circles are the Martyrs, Confessors and Virgins; and in this way others appear in the distance in groups veiled by transparent splendours, without creating any confusion.[94] In the same church he painted on the exterior of the organ shutters Christ worshipped by the Magi, and with them their knights holding hawks and servants with rich gifts; and on the inside the Doctors which with their pens defended the Church militant, and above angels singing their praises;[95] and below the organ case he represented God the Father surrounded by many small cherubs. He worked on the second for Girolamo Grimani, Procurator of Saint Mark's, for the main chapel of the church of San Giuseppe with the birth of the Messiah with the shepherds around the crib; and two angels descending from Heaven with a brief inscription in their hands: *Gloria in excelsis Deo*;[96] and another he painted some time before of the Transfiguration on Mount Tabor, which can be seen in print.[97]

94. Accademia, Venice  95. Pinacoteca di Brera, Milan
96. Still in situ  97. Accademia, Venice

In San Luca there is the third one with the saint seated on the ox in the act of writing the Gospel, who looks at the Virgin, who appears to him in the sky, who can also be seen portrayed in a small panel in the same room together with the tools of painting.[98] Fortunate painter, you who were worthy of happily portraying the eyes of that divine countenance, and therefore learned the way of composing divine Ideas. The fourth, which is in truth one of artist's best, is in the sacristy of San Zaccaria, with Our Lady above in the middle of decorated architectures, with Saints Catherine and Francis below and the young John who presents a purple cross to the seraphic saint. There is Saint Jerome on the other side dressed as a cardinal, who could not be painted with further decorum or naturalness, and for whom the artist used a real portrait.[99]

The fifth in Santa Maria Maggiore of the Assumption of the Virgin with an unusual design, and a balustrade around the sepulchre, where the apostles are placed;[100] and hanging on the walls are paintings of the Adulteress, the Centurion, and of

98. Still in situ 99. Accademia, Venice 100. Accademia, Venice

*Opposite: The Virgin and Child with Saints Catherine, Francis, John the Baptist, Jerome and Joseph (Pala Bonaldi), ca. 1562*

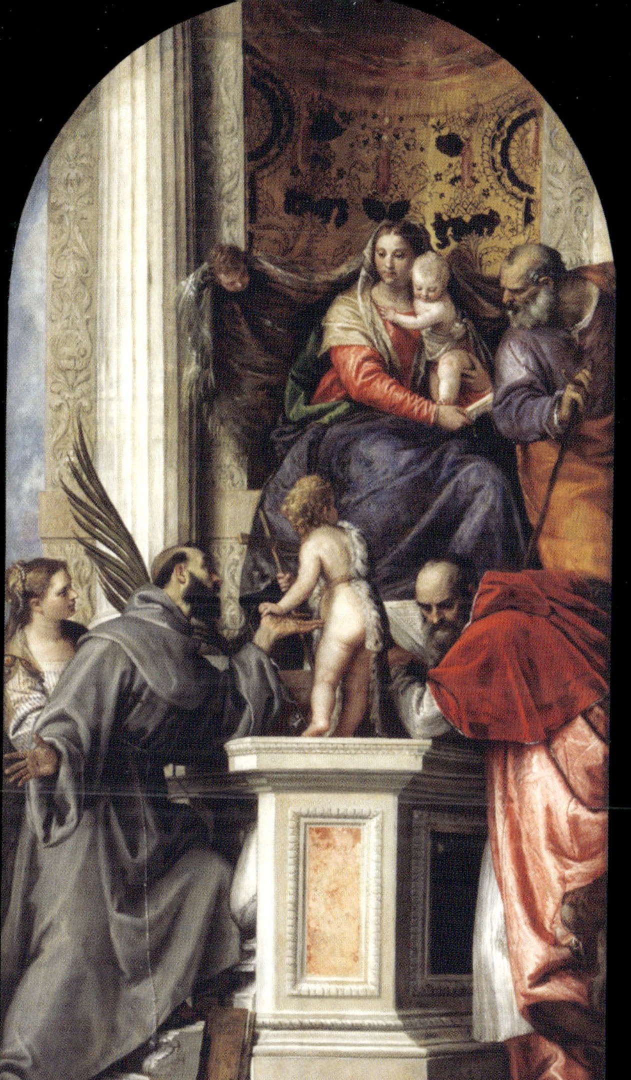

the sons of Zebedee brought by their mother to Christ;[101] and another of the Agony in the Garden, with Our Lord held up by a most beautiful angel, leaning on a column.[102]

But let us for a moment move away from Venice; for the high altar of the church of San Jacopo in Murano Veronese once again painted the Saviour with Zebedee's wife and the two brothers James and John, for whom she asks for the left and the right place in the Kingdom of Heaven, and to her Christ answered that before that could come to pass, the chalice of suffering must be drunk.[103]

In another is the Virgin, who greets her sister-in-law Elizabeth at the head of a staircase;[104] and in the third the victorious Redeemer rises from the sepulchre surrounded by an array of celebrating angels, having overcome Satan, and having removed his prey, the Holy Fathers, from Hell;[105] and on the organ he painted the marriage of Saint Catherine Martyr, and Saints James and Augustine.[106]

101. Possibly in Grenoble, Musée des Beaux-Arts 102. Pinacoteca di Brera, Milan 103. Burghley House 104. Barber Institute of Fine Arts, Birmingham 105. Chelsea and Westminster Hospital, London 106. The exterior panels of the organ shutters with the Mystic Marriage of Saint Catherine are now lost. The interior ones, with Saints James and Augustine are at Burghley House.

In San Pietro Martire he worked for the Compagnia del Rosario on the painting over the benches next to the altar, with the Virgin in the air, the Pope, cardinals and princes on one side, on the other matrons with their young daughters, to whom Saint Dominic distributes vermillion roses gathered by a companion from the nearby hedge. Precious roses, gathered with devoted affection by a pious believer, you have the virtue of curing the soul infected by error, from your sweet scents are produced those perfumes, which rising to Heaven from a devout heart are able to placate divine indignation.[107]

And in a small chapel near the Angeli there is a Saint Jerome in meditation,[108] and above a door Saint Agatha visited in prison by Saint Peter, and an angel precedes him with a torch.[109]

Not far away in Torcello, city buried among its ruins, in the Church of Sant'Antonio there is the altarpiece in the main chapel with the abbot saint placed in between two bishops, and a young page holds for him a book.[110] In the organ he painted the Annunciation and the Adoration of the Magi, and other small stories of the Virgin in grisaille, on the

107. Museo Vetrario, Murano, Venice 108. San Pietro Martire, Murano, Venice 109. San Pietro Martire, Murano, Venice 110. Pinacoteca di Brera, Milan

organ case;[111] and on the sides he depicted in nine pictures episodes of Saint Cristina in like style.[112]

In the first that Virgin Saint is persuaded by her father to worship idols. Then having broken to pieces the gold and silver idols, she gives them to the poor. Subsequently she is beaten with sticks by henchmen on her father's orders. Then she is put in prison and is visited by the angel. And afterwards brought in front of her father, and persevering in her faith in Christ, she is stripped naked and tortured with hooks, and placed over a wheel under which a fire is lit. Again shut in a prison, and healed by angels, she is then thrown into a lake, is baptized, and picked up in a boat by fishermen.

In Mazzorbo, an adjoining small island, in the church of Santa Caterina there is the altarpiece with Saint Nicholas and with him other saints and portraits of nuns.[113] And to follow the path as far as Zara, in San Domenico there is the canvas of the Rosary; and in Lecce, a city in Puglia, the people there take pleasure in two figures of Saint Philip and James by this pre-eminent hand.

111. Museo Provinciale, Torcello, Venice 112. Four are in the Museo Provinciale, Torcello, Venice; two in the Staatsgalerie, Stuttgart; one in the Accademia Carrara, Bergamo; two are lost. 113. In fact Saint Benedict with other Saints, in Palazzo Pitti, Florence.

But it is time to turn our sails towards Venice, after having travelled a distance on the sea, and briefly we will describe the last works painted by Paolo, with which he gloriously sealed the end of his life.

He had later painted in San Nicolò dei Frari four scenes, depicting the Baptism of Christ with most beautiful angels;[114] the Supper which he had with the disciples; the same crucified on Calvary with the Magdalene and Longinus at the foot of the cross, repenting of his error;[115] the Saviour resurrected from the sepulchre, surrounded by blessed spirits, with soldiers woken by the light of the splendours; then again he depicted in the middle of the ceiling the Magi worshipping the Messiah, adorned with beautiful clothes, and with a background of noble architectures, and there is a servant, who holds a horse majestic in its appearance, eager in his attitude and so lively in movement that it seems he is coming out of the canvas.[116] At the sides he painted in one of the compartments Saint Nicholas, who was elected to the bishopric of Myra, being venerated by the clergy;[117] and in the other Saint Francis on Mount La Verna is stigmatised in the test of Love by the

114. Pinacoteca di Brera, Milan 115. Accademia, Venice
116. SS. Giovanni e Paolo, Venice 117. Accademia, Venice

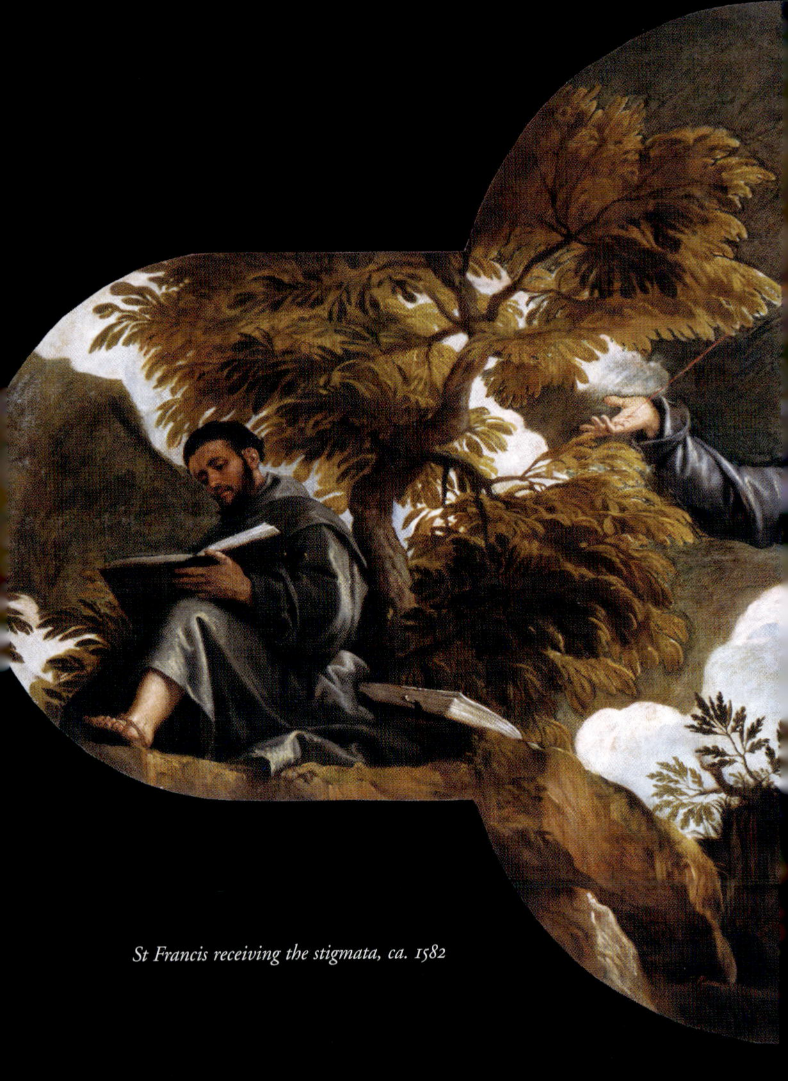

*St Francis receiving the stigmata, ca. 1582*

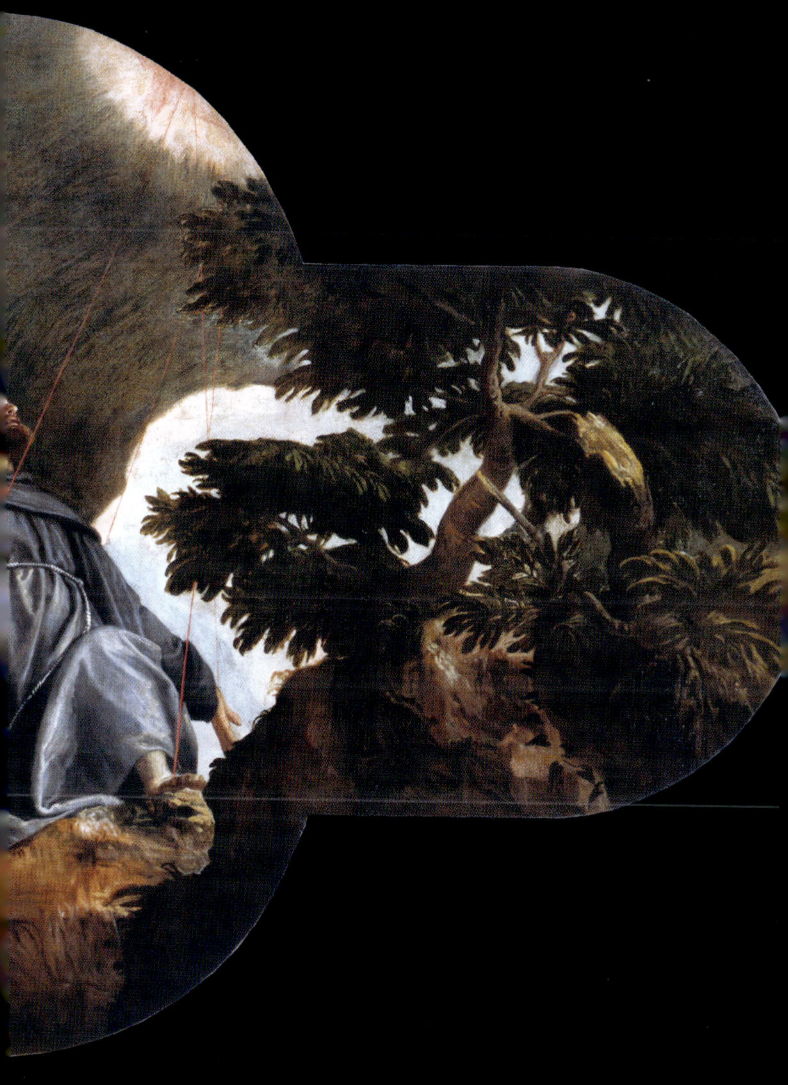

Seraphim;[118] and the Evangelists in the corners.[119]

Around that same time it was decided by the Senate, that the paintings in the Hall of the Collegio should be finished, which were divided between Tintoretto and Paolo; to whom was given among these the painting over the tribune, in which he painted Doge Sebastiano Venier, one of the most famous heroes ever to command the Venetian army, whom he depicted only from his imagination, decked out with a golden cloak, kneeling in front of the Saviour, giving thanks for the victory over the Turks as commander of the Venetian forces, to whom groups of angels bring palms and olive branches as a sign of triumph and for the peace brought to the homeland.[120] There are with him Faith with her chalice, Venice holding hands with Saint Justina with the palm, on whose blessed feast day, when she gloriously ascended to Heaven for her martyrdom, the Venetian armies triumphed over the Ottoman king; and he also portrayed there Agostino Barbarigo, the Provveditore, who during the conflict died gloriously fighting, and because of whose prudence the allies remained united.

In the first compartment over the tribune he

118. Accademia, Venice 119. SS. Giovanni e Paolo, Venice
120. Still in situ

depicted Venice enthroned, Justice who offers her the sword, and Peace the olive branch, because she has always ruled her Empire with utmost fairness;[121] with these letters next to it: *Custodes libertatis.**

In the middle he painted Faith in contemplation in the sky, and underneath the representation of a sacrifice, to signify the uncorrupted religion of that republic, nourished by divine service,[122] and above it is written: *Nunquam derelicta.*§ And at the bottom one can read: *Reipublicæ Fundamentum.*†

And in the third compartment are Neptune with the trident and Mars standing over instruments of war, with putti flying in the sky, carrying helmets and sea shells, which refer to Venice's powerful dominion over the earth and the sea,[123] with the inscription: *Robur Imperij.*‡

In the groups on either side he disposed the eight moral Virtues, Fidelity, Eloquence, Concord, Vigilance, Secrecy and others that are suitable to the governing of states.[124]

And among them in some ovals coloured in green

* The Guardians of Liberty § Never Abandoned
† The Foundation of the Republic ‡ The Strength of the Empire

121. Still in situ 122. Still in situ 123. Still in situ
124. Still in situ

are painted the stories of Scylla, Decius, Alexander, Zaleucus, and around the walls he depicted others in red in a frieze in compartments with David, Solon, Archimedes, Claudius, Leonidas, with many putti in between.[125]

In the ceiling of the ante-chamber he did a new painting in fresco of Venice with many figures before her, carrying various ecclesiastical insignia, and a boy who holds a mitre, and on either side is a cornucopia to signify the abundance of the income of the state.[126]

Towards the end of his life Paolo painted in the Hall of the Great Council the return of Doge Andrea Contarini to Venice, having vanquished the Genoese at Chioggia, which after a long siege was reduced to the extremity of misery, and surrendered to the mercy of the prince, who was the general of the Venetian forces; who, having brought with him three thousand of them with other prisoners (who were subsequently freed), paraded in triumph in Saint Mark's Square; and here he is seen being greeted by the senators, who obsequiously kneel in front of him, as a saviour of the homeland and vanquisher of the enemies.[127] There is the Primo Cereo of Saint Mark's, the clerics of the Seminary with the cross and silver maces in front of

125. Still in situ 126. Still in situ 127. Still in situ

them, so life-like as if he had portrayed them one by one from life. Around the piazza are also scattered soldiers and standard-bearers, and Marco Dolce, Captain of Justice, portrayed from life, who even in painting brings terror to the wicked.

Near the stone of the proclamations he represented Greeks, Dalmatians and Gypsies mingling together, and among these a galley slave depicted with great realism. There are furthermore weapons on the floor and two most lively dogs; which things Paolo used generally to do mainly from his imagination only.

And though one cannot fully praise such an outstanding painting with a short discussion, we can demonstrate its perfection from the fact that he inscribed his name on it (being in this always modest) to explain that this was one of his most exceptional works, and above it are inscribed in marble these words:

Andreas Contareno Dux,
Qui Clodianæ classis Imperator,
Servata Patria, atrocissimos hostes
Felicissime debellavit. MCCCLXVIII.
Vixit postea Annos XIV.*

*The Doge Andrea Contarini, in command of the Clodian fleet, saved the fatherland by successfully fighting its bitter enemies. 1368. He lived thereafter for fourteen years.

But let us also talk about the works that Veronese painted on commission for princes and lords, from which it will be possible to understand the universal taste that everyone had for his paintings, which will be recounted as they come to hand, rather than in chronological order, since they were painted over a long period during which his manner did not change very much.

For the Emperor Rudolph II he painted three inventions, of Venus and Mars; of Cephalus who, deceived by Air, killed his wife; and the same Goddess dressing her hair, adorning it with flowers while Cupid holds her mirror.

To Carlo Duke of Savoy he sent a large canvas[128] depicting the Queen of Sheba before Solomon, followed by courtiers and servants, who bring rich gifts; and another of David, who was cut off the head of proud Goliath, and both of these were displayed in the gallery in Turin.

For Duke Guglielmo of Mantua he painted in a medium-size picture Moses as a child rescued from the river, after the daughter of Pharaoh took pity on him, accompanied by two of her maids dressed in such pretty clothes, that silk was never seen resplen-

128. Galleria Sabauda, Turin

dent with such lively colours, which was judged to be the most remarkable among the paintings of the gallery of Mantua. And at Artimino, the retreat of the Grand Duke of Tuscany, are four paintings of scenes from the scriptures.

Four large canvases are owned by the Duke of Modena; exceptional amongst these one with the Saviour worshipped by the Magi; in another the Marriage at Cana in Galilee with women at the table portrayed from life; Christ on his way to Calvary followed by many soldiers and henchmen, the Virgin Our Lady with the Maries; and in the fourth is the Virgin again, seated next to whom is Faith with her chalice and the cross in her hand with some portraits in front of them.[129]

Many were the paintings collected by great men after the painter's death. Monsignor Gessi, who was later cardinal, while he was nuncio in Venice, sent to His Holiness Pope Paul V the marriage of Saint Catherine Martyr with a numerous cortège of truly celestial angels.

Prince Borghese has a medium-size painting with Saint Anthony who preaches on the beach to the fish, which jump out of the water to listen to him, as

129. All four in the Gemaldëgalerie, Dresden

if they truly understood him.[130]

Two canvases are owned by Prince Ludovisi: the purification of Our Lady, and Saint John who preaches to the multitude;[131] and the Marchese Giustiniani has a figure of the dead Christ supported by two angels;[132] and the Count of Monterrey, who used to be viceroy of Naples, had two stories from Ovid.

Basil, Viscount Fielding, an Englishman, and a few years ago ambassador in Venice, bought many pictures by his hand, including the following inventions:

A composition of the Virgin with the martyr Catherine life-size. In other medium-size pictures Eve, who was feeding Abel and Cain as small children in the wilderness with food from the trees and water from the running rivulets;[133] Abraham in the act of sacrificing his son Isaac; Our Lord worshipped by the Magi;[134] the same being baptized; afterwards flagellated at the column, with the event represented at night, and the scene receives light from a lit torch; the resurrected Saviour;[135] and Saint John preaching to the crowds; a small subject of Our Lady with two nuns;[136] another with the Lord invited by Martha and

130. Galleria Borghese, Rome 131. Galleria Borghese, Rome
132. Gemäldegalerie, Berlin 133. Kunsthistorisches Museum, Vienna
134. Kunsthistorisches Museum, Vienna 135. Kunsthistorisches Museum, Vienna 136. Kunsthistorisches Museum, Vienna

Mary into their house, accompanied by the apostles; Queen Esther in front of Ahasuerus with a following of many ladies.[137]

Of mythological subjects, there was a life-size Venus and Adonis, who was leaning over the goddess's face holding his dogs; and in two small canvases Nessus the centaur shot with arrows by Hercules for having kidnapped his wife, and with a different invention, Venus delighting in the beautiful Adonis;[138] which works were seen mainly among the collection of paintings of Bartolomeo della Nave.

Monsieur de Housset, previously French ambassador to Venice, also bought the martyrdom of Saint Justina, the conversion of the Magdalene, and a resurrected Christ in an octagon, which Paolo painted in competition with a Birth of Christ by Bassano and a Deposition from the Cross by Tintoretto; and a new composition of Adonis with the amorous goddess and Cupid, who keeps hold of a hound.[139]

For the contemplation of Jacopo Contarini he painted a picture of about four *braccia* with Europa seated over the deceiving bull, who lovingly kisses her foot, licking it with his tongue.[140] Some of her maids

137. Galleria degli Uffizi, Florence 138. Kunsthistorisches Museum, Vienna 139. Seattle Art Museum, Seattle 140. Doge's Palace, Venice

serve her as support; others decorate her with flowers; and cupids fly over her scattering flowers. And he represented that event extraordinarily well, precisely as it is described by Ovid, whose verses translated sound like this in our language:

Poscia l'ardita e regia giovinetta
Non sapendo d'un Dio premer' il dorso,
Sopra si vede, ed egli humile in tanto
Si leva, e verso il mare a poco a poco
Si drizza, e immerge il falso pie nell'acque;
Indi per mezzo il mar la ricca preda
Lieto sen porta; ed ella, che si vede
Fuggir il lido, da timor oppressa
Di rugiadose perle bagna il viso,
E temendo restar nel mar sommersa,
Con una man l'uno dei corni afferra,
E con l'altra sul dorso si riposa.
In tanto gli aurei crini e 'l nobil velo
Mossi venian dall'aura in bei raggiri.*

* At last Europa knowing not (for so the Maide was calde)/ On whome she venturde for to ride, was nerawhit appalde/To set hir selfe upon his backe. Then by and by the God/ From maine drie land to maine moyst Sea gan leysurly to plod./ At first he did but dip his feete within the outmost wave,/ And backe againe, then further in another plunge he gave./ And so still further till at the last he had his wished pray/Amid the deepe where was no meanes to scape

In this fashion Paolo represented in several places the beautiful Europa, who weeps as she finally crosses the sea, not knowing that she is protected by a god. Beauty is a ray which blinds anyone who fixes his gaze on it, and on which graces and favours are bestowed in tribute, so that in a short time we will see her tears dry, once she is made lady of the noblest part of the world. The lordly state draws a veil over every error, and vice is only pointed out in the beggarly if ever it is mendacious.

In a much larger canvas belonging to the Pisani family he represented the Constancy of Alexander with the women of the defeated Darius, when Fortune, having opened the road to the crown of Persia, encircled his temples with immortal laurel who put to flight such a large army with few losses amongst his men.[141] Here you can see the mother, the wives and the daughters of Darius kneeling at his feet entrusting themselves to his clemency, who generously desired that they should be respected and served as

with life away./The Ladie quaking all for feare with rufull countnance cast/ Ay toward shore from whence she came, held with hir righthand fast/ One of his hornes: and with the left did stay upon his backe./The weather flaskt and whisked up hir garments being slacke. Ovid, *Metamorphoses* Bk II, translated by Arthur Golding.

141. National Gallery, London

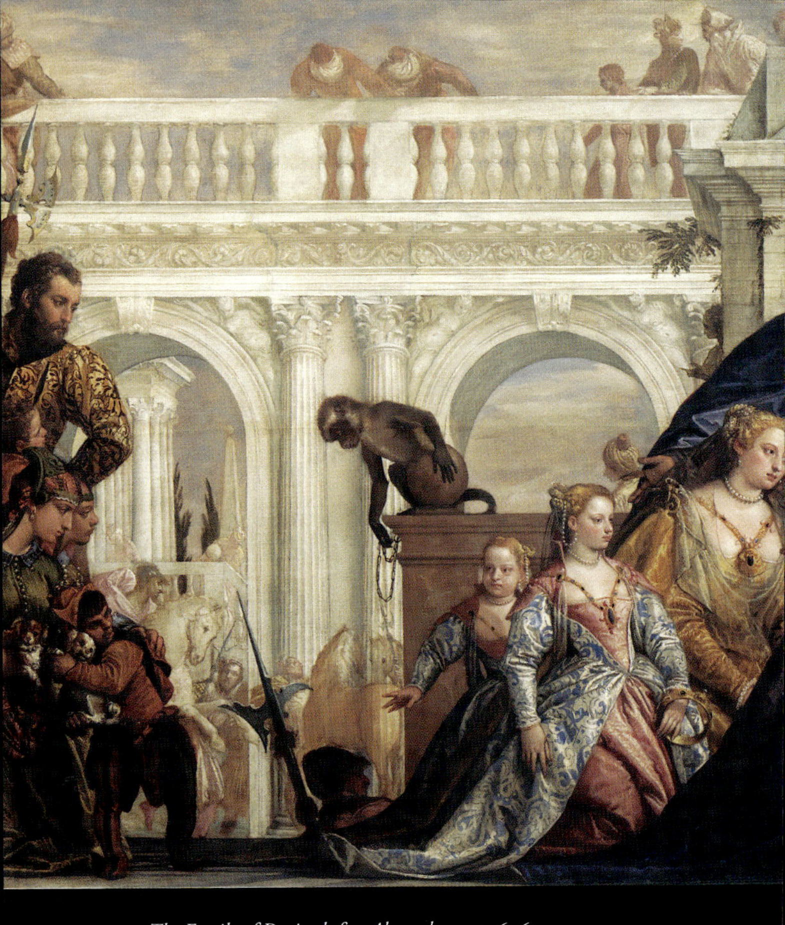

*The Family of Darius before Alexander, ca. 1565-67*

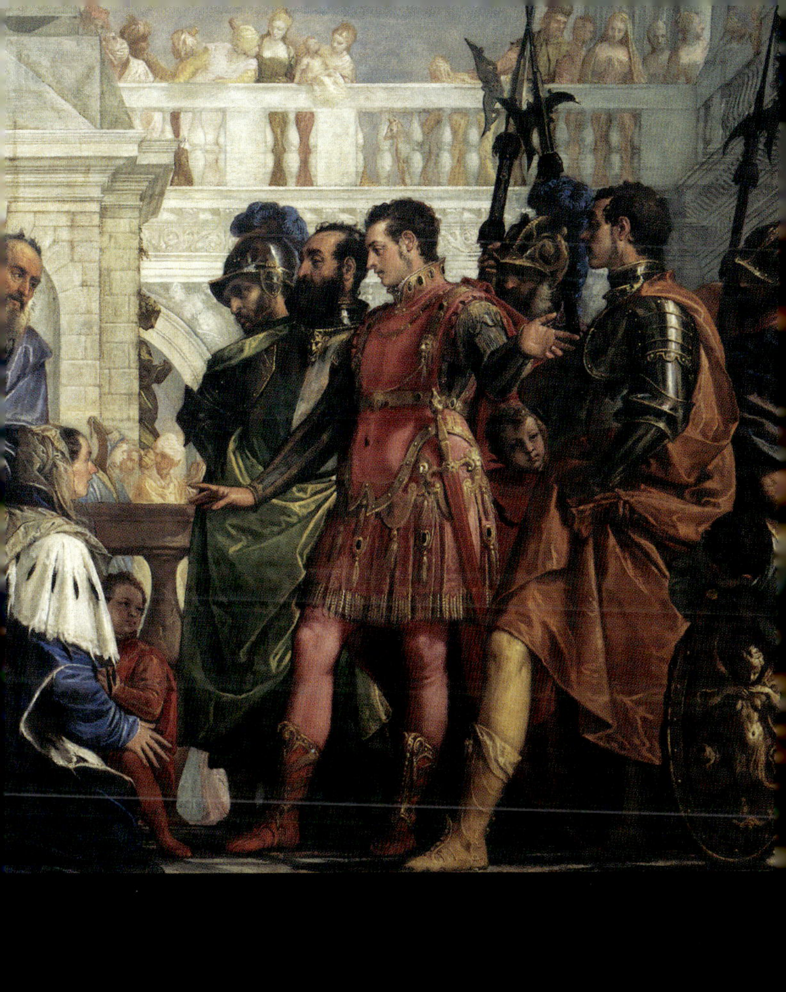

queens. There is on one side Hephæstion, his favourite captain, and other knights, who admire such magnanimity, badly imitated by the captains of the armies to whom slaughter and theft serve as trophies of victories. Many witnesses to the generous action look out from the windows and the balconies.

The Procurator Da Pesaro has a small painting with Our Lord brought down from the cross, lying on his mother's knees, with the lamenting sisters, Nicodemus and Joseph, who in a grief-stricken manner give him the last offices, but above all the Magdalene, pierced by the pain, inundates his feet with tears, affixing on them her doleful kisses.

Cavalier Gussoni has the painting of Susannah; and in the gallery of the Senator Domenico Ruzini one can see Our Lord shown by Pilate to the people, in which the painter worked hard to imitate the appearance of a most delicate body when it is wounded, and in it can be seen, so to speak, even the blood pulsing through the limbs and the blushing of the face caused by shame, as will happen to a noble person, who suffers through no fault of his own. In another canvas is the finding of Moses as a child, differently composed from the ones we mentioned, where the daughter of Pharaoh orders her maid that he should be cared for, and he seems to smile; in the meantime an old woman opens a cloth to wrap him in it; which painting does not need further praise as it is well known.

In the houses of the Cornaro family in the parish of San Cassiano are two religious paintings and two moral compositions; a painting of the Adulteress in the Soranzo family; the Adoration of the Magi and the Centurion praying the Saviour to heal his servant in the house of Vincenzo Grimani of Sant' Ermacora;[142] and another composition of the Visit of the Magi with many small figures is in the Mocenigo Palace at San Samuele; the portrait of Onofrio Giustiniani, who was commander of the galleys at the battle of Lepanto, created knight by the Senate when he brought the happy news of the victory against the Turks, is in the houses of the Giustiniani family at San Moisè; and with Giovan Battista Sanuto we find two paintings of Venus, who having given birth to Anteros, shows him to Eros, held by Mercury and served by the Graces; as the poets claim that Anteros creates that affinity which nourishes love, without which he would quickly die;[143] of Megara the daughter of Creon of Thebes, who

142. Nelson-Atkins Museum of Art, Kansas City
143. Galleria degli Uffizi, Florence

shows him her son Ophites saved from Hercules' fury, when on his way back from hell, he had killed Creontiades, Therimachus and Deicoön, her other children; and a composition of Virtue in the form of an old woman crowned with laurel, and of Lust, and between them he placed a young boy of that family, while both figures invite him towards themselves.[144] A man born amongst comforts and delights will only resist the force of the senses with difficulty, and so will often deviate from the path of virtue.

And Francesco Michiel of Sant'Angelo has the Purification of the Virgin, whose beautiful face inspires grace and devotion, and the scene is filled with beautiful architecture and portraits of his family.

A painting of the marriage of the Virgin Mary to Saint Joseph celebrated by the high priest in the temple is with Marco Ottoboni, Grand Chancellor of Venice.

Nicolò Crasso has the portrait of one of his family. Bernardo Giunti has two portraits on the same canvas. Four scenes of Judith,[145] Susannah,[146] Rachel[147] and Esther[148] were with the Bonaldi family at Sant'Eustachio.

Monsignor Melchiori, parish priest of Santa

144. Museo del Prado, Madrid 145. Musée des Beaux-Arts, Caen 146. Musée du Louvre, Paris 147. Musée National du Château, Versailles 148. Musée du Louvre, Paris

Fosca, can take pleasure in the representation of a miracle of the Virgin that happened to the daughter of a king of France, who was emperor too, who being envied by her stepmother for her beauty, was sent by her out of the city to be killed by servants; these, taking pity on her for the prayers that she offered the Virgin, only cut off her hands and brought them back to the evil woman as a sign of having obeyed her orders. But the son of a duke coming from the hunt, having heard the noise and having witnessed the miserable spectacle, had the girl brought to the city, and tended there; and falling in love with her beauty he then married her.

It happened then that, passing through the imperial court, because of certain festivities proclaimed by the emperor at his wife's suggestion (to alleviate the pain of having lost his daughter), he stayed there for a while, giving proof in many ways of his worth. Now he heard from his father that his wife had given birth to two children. When the empress discovered this from the messenger, and because she had discovered that the girl was her own step-daughter whose hands were cut, she intercepted the prince's answer, which warmly entrusted his wife with her

*Overleaf: Youth of the Sanuto Family between Virtue and Vice, ca. 1580*

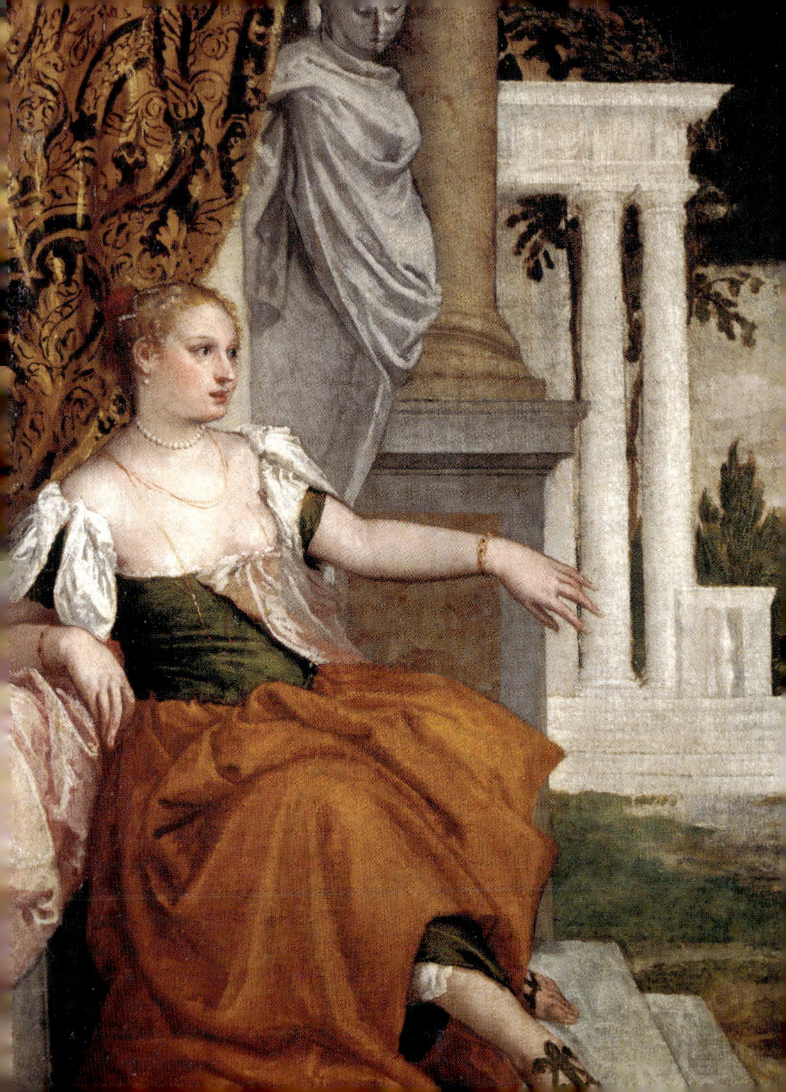

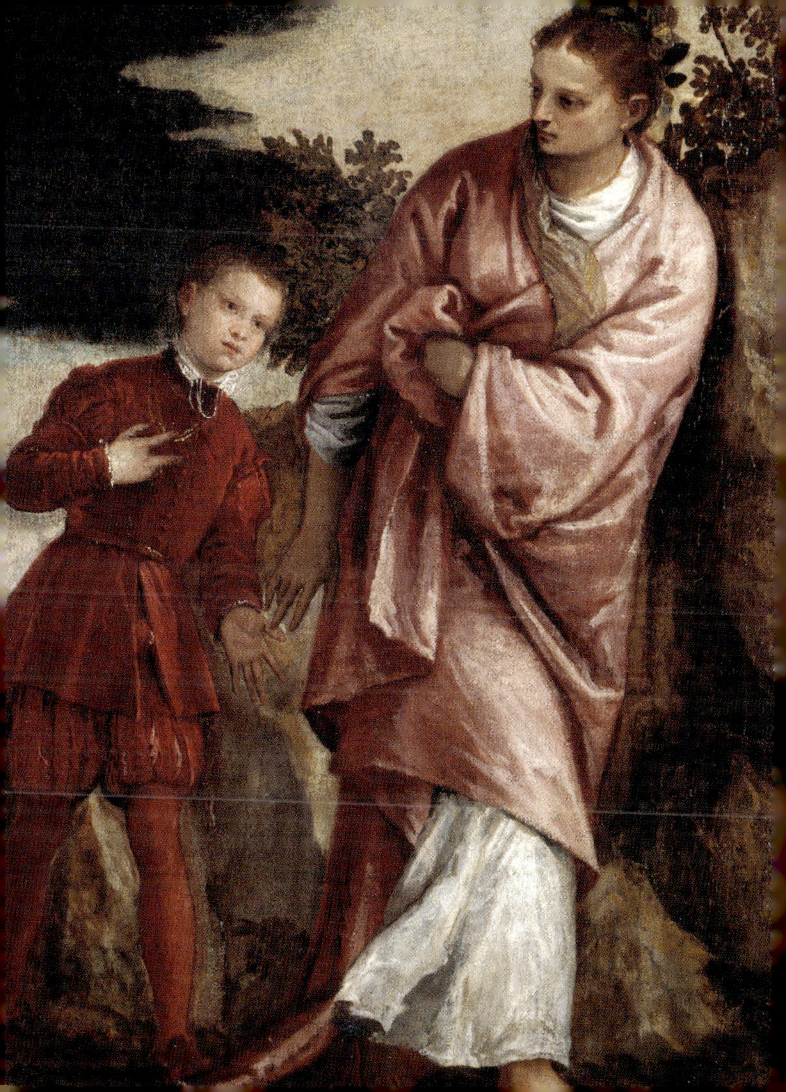

two children to his father, and changed the meaning of it, begging him if he loved him to kill the wife as an adulteress and the children too.

The duke's order was followed, and she was sent with the grandchildren to the forest to be devoured by wild beasts; and while she was wandering in those solitudes she was found by a hermit and she lived with him for a while, often recommending herself to Our Lady's protection, who soon after appeared to her and gave her back her hands, freeing her from that suffering.

When the prince returned home and heard what had happened to his beloved wife against his orders, he immediately set off to find her in the wilderness; and he brought her back to court with a great celebration. Having heard from her whose daughter she was (which she had kept hidden until then) he told the emperor straight away, who had the wicked wife who had been the cause of such evil burnt at the stake.

Here you see the Virgin Mary who appears to the young girl in the forest, lying on a miserable little bed with her twins on the side, and two angels hold her hands in a piece of cloth, representing this unhappy condition with great compassion.[149]

149. Staatliche Kunstsammlungen, Kassel

In the gallery of Jan Reynst in Venice (of whom we have written elsewhere), two portraits of a married couple of the Soranzo family can be admired; the parable of the Samaritan, the model of Christian mercy (without which every work is in vain), who having dismounted from his horse in the middle of a wood heals his wounds, pouring oil and wine, a scene very well depicted for the weakness shown in the wounded man and for the care of the Samaritan;[150] the resurrected Saviour covered with a linen cloth, in a small painting, encircled by many flying angels, with a brief inscription held by some of the winged ones, on which is written: *Ego et pater unum sumus**; which can be said to be gems of priceless value; and the Sacrifice of Abraham.

He also sent to his house in Amsterdam a painting by this artist of Saint Catherine marrying Christ, with delightful angels who celebrate the royal wedding with the sound of lutes, and in it can be seen distant buildings this is one of Paolo's most precious works.

The family of Count Vidman owns three paintings of the Paralytic, of Lazarus resurrected and of Saint Paul converted, with many figure, and a

* I and my father are one. John 10,30

150. Gemaldëgalerie, Dresden

charming composition of the Virgin with the Child in her lap, with the Baptist kissing His sweet foot, Saint Joseph on one side, who leans on his right arm, and the martyr Catherine who admires her husband and lord, all of them praiseworthy figures.[151]

Paolo del Sera has the martyrdom of the said saint, who prays to Heaven while the angel destroys the instrument of her torture with a sword; and Cristoforo Orsetti has the figure of Saint Stephen praying.

And he also has an invention of Mars, who amuses himself with Venus, and Cupid holds his horse by the reins, in truth a prized painting.[152]

Giovanni and Jacopo Van Veerle have in their houses the portrait of a merchant wearing robes, who places a pair of glasses on a table. A gladiator dressed in white with a broadsword in his hand and the letters *Nec spe nec metu.**[153] Another portrait of a woman holding a small book, and an extraordinary one of a Dalmatian.

Also in Venice with the Nani family at the Giudecca are certain spalliere painted by Paolo and commissioned by Marcantonio Barbaro, Procurator

* Without hope or fear

151. Galleria degli Uffizi, Florence 152. Galleria Sabauda, Turin
153. Palacio Real, Madrid. Now attributed to Antonio Badile.

of Saint Mark's, who would for his own pleasure copy out the draperies from the cartoons drawn by Paolo, and then once they were put together, Paolo would colour them in with oil.

So in seven sections, divided by arches and Corinthian columns, he painted the story of the Hebrew maiden Esther, who attained the royal throne of Persia from slavery. No noose holds more strongly than beauty, which turns kings to its own will, and examples are not lacking in both sacred and profane books. That daughter of Abihail, brother of Mordecai of the stock of Benjamin, brought to Babylon by Nebuchadnezzar in the captivity of Jeconiah, king of Judah, who was living then in Shushan, the capital of Persia, was raised as a daughter by her uncle.

Now in the third year of his reign Ahasuerus held sumptuous banquets for his main captains and their servants to celebrate his magnificence, setting the tables in front of the royal gardens underneath rich tents of different colours, held by ropes in Tyrian dye and purple, inserted in silver rings attached to marble columns. And carpets fringed in gold were placed over the floor made out of emeralds and Parian marble, and the table was set with lavish foods, while precious nectars were drunk in gilt cups.

In the first compartment we see generals and captains at the banquet dressed in beautiful costumes in the Persian manner, and among them is the portrait of the Procurator himself. There are servants who bring food, and give the guests to drink; and in a corner is the steward with a stick in his hand, and on another side a woman with a cushion under her side, giving orders; and in the distance can be seen the royal gardens.

In the second one King Ahasuerus sits at the banquet under a rich tent among the most important generals, Carshena, Shethar, Admatha, Tarshish, Meres, Marsena and Memucan, the only ones that were allowed to set eyes upon the king's face and sit next to him. And having heard their advice with regard to what should be done with Queen Vashti who, having been invited by him did not come to the solemn banquet, he agreed with Memucan's suggestion to repudiate her, to suppress the freedom of wives, and elect a new queen. The meat-carver is in front of the king, and other servants serve him various foods in silver plates; a soldier with a halberd stands at the threshold under the arch.

In the third one, after the royal decree has been carried out by the ministers, and the most beautiful maidens of the empire have been assembled, and given in custody to Hegai the eunuch who guarded the king's women, and who was in charge of taking care of everything they needed, Esther walks towards the king adorned with every beauty and enriched with veils and gems, and she goes piercing hearts with her gaze, and she leans on two handsome maids dressed in livery. A young page holds the hem of her dress, another one places a cushion in front of her, and she is followed by two old matrons; and in the distance from balconies many observers wonder at her beauty.

In the fourth one Mordecai, dressed as a servant, tells the king about the conspiracy of the eunuchs Bigthan and Teresh; and subsequently they are justly punished, as is mentioned in the annals. Many satraps next to the king witness the scene, and a servant stands outside the room with a hawk on his hand, to which he gives the heart of an animal to eat.

In the fifth one Ahasuerus appears again among the generals under a green baldachin, dressed in purple with a gold coat and a barbarian ornament on his head made out of bands decorated with gems. Before him a reverential scribe is reading from the annals about the conspiracy discovered by Mordecai. And then the king introduces Haman, son of Hammedatha of the stock of Agag, whom he had placed over the princes of his empire (and who had hurried to court to petition the king for Mordecai's death, because he was annoyed that he had not received from him the homage he felt was his due). After hearing from Haman how a friend of the king should be honoured (as Haman believed he was to receive a new honour), Ahasuerus commands him to dress Mordecai in the royal cloak, with a crown on his head, and to bring him across the city on a finely caparisoned horse, cheering him as the king's friend. You can imagine how the envious man was astonished as there is no greater sting than seeing one's enemy elevated to greatness. And in that painting there is a dwarf, holding a dog, and another is lying at the king's feet, as Paolo often included similar animals in his compositions.

In the sixth one, Esther having been told by her uncle about Haman's persecution, has presented herself to the king dressed as splendidly as possible. Reassured by the touch of the royal sceptre (as entry the the royal presence was forbidden), and guaranteeing his continued graciousness by her manners and glances, she invites him to dine with her and Haman; the king, Haman and the queen can be seen at the table; and having heard Esther denounce Haman as an enemy and traitor, and being even more greatly angered by having seen Haman lie down on her bed, Ahasuerus orders that Haman should be hanged at the gallows that had been prepared for Mordecai. In this way the greatness of the king's minister came to an end, and with all suddenness his felicity was transformed into infamous death. There is no fortune more subject to mutability than that of a favourite. The graces of the great are as gaping graves for courtiers.

In the seventh painting Ahasuerus, leaving the table, walks towards his rooms, and Esther walks down the stairs with her servants by another route. Nearby stand a dwarf with two parrots, and a soldier with a halberd, and there is a distant prospect of royal palaces.

And in the same palace are certain covers for carriages painted with fanciful images and coat-of-arms by Paolo.

And briefly to pick up the thread of Paolo's public works: in a small room of the Fondaco dei Tedeschi he painted in competition with other painters four curious compositions. In one the world is represented as a great sphere with the zodiac around it; at the top is Saturn with the sickle, further down is Religion dressed in blue, and a boy holds the crozier, and another putto squares and compass; and at the feet of the World lies a wrinkled old woman on a mean little bed who represents Heresy.[154]

In the second one Germany is portrayed as a noble Lady with crown and sceptre, to whom Jupiter confers the imperial crown, royal crowns and a multitude of gems, held by two delightful children.[155] In the third one Pallas and Mars stand for military discipline, as is practiced by that bellicose nation.[156] Juno and the Sun are in the fourth one and signify the quantity of mines of gold and other metals, with which that region abounds.[157]

In the last years of his life Paolo painted for the Lanaiuoli in the church of San Pantaleon a large canvas with an arched top showing Saint Bernardino, when he was in the world, who working in a hospital in Siena at a time of plague, gives orders suitable to that place, distributes alms and heals the sick; graces that are only bestowed on those who piously serve Heaven.[158] And for the Patriarch Trevisani he painted in the church of Castello the altarpiece of the Apostle Saints Peter, Paul and John;[159] the

154. Kaiser Friedrich Museum, Berlin; destroyed in 1945
155. Kaiser Friedrich Museum, Berlin; destroyed in 1945
156. Kaiser Friedrich Museum, Berlin; destroyed in 1945
157. Kaiser Friedrich Museum, Berlin; destroyed in 1945
158. Still in situ 159. San Pietro di Castello, Venice

Annunciation in the Scuola dei Mercanti,[160] and the Assumption of the Virgin for the ceiling of the refectory of the Fathers of San Jacopo at Giudecca.[161]

Finally let us discuss the paintings that remained in Paolo's house after his death, now owned by Giuseppe Caliari his grandson and only remaining heir of that family. A picture extraordinarily painted with the dead Saviour on the Eternal Father's knees, who explains to him the Love that had caused him to die for mankind. Flanking them are two weeping angels, and cherubs decorated with wings illuminated with many colours fly around; a wonderful painting for the science demonstrated in the body of the Saviour, knowledgeably depicted.

In two minor canvases are painted the mystery of the Incarnation, and the beauty of the Virgin, the loveliness of the angel and the decoration of that noble room cannot be described in full; in the other Saint Catherine Martyr married to Christ, in whose beautiful face her pure affections can be discovered.[162]

In another painting eight feet long there is the Judgment of Solomon, with the two women fighting over the living child, and in the true mother is

160. Accademia, Venice 161. Accademia, Venice
162. Royal Collection, London

expressed the pain which it is likely she would experience in feeling her flesh being divided, while the executioner in a peculiar costume with naked arms is in the act of carrying out the royal decree.[163] In another is the Adoration of the Magi with a curious invention; the figure of Saint Mary Magdalene in three quarters length meditating on a crucifix, and placing her right hand over a skull that signifies the fate of all men. Judith in half figure who, having cut off Holofernes's head, places it in the bag carried by her old maid.[164] Susannah at her bath with the two old men enamoured of her, who look at her from the bushes; and another standing figure of the Magdalene who looks up to Heaven. The Marriage of Saint Catherine Martyr, and Saint Anne who unrolls a cloth.[165] The Nativity of the Saviour; and His Prayers in the Garden, in small format, painted with exceptional refinement. The same at the column; and a delightful composition with a Venetian gentleman of the Mocenigo family who having returned from the hunt plays the viola, with gods and cupids, passing from the enjoyments of the woods to those of the Virtues.

He also owns two long canvases that Paolo

163. Freeman Collection, Detroit 164. Kunshistorisches Museum, Vienna 165. Hermitage, St Petersburg

painted for the Senate, which were to be used to weave tapestries for the Collegio; in one[166] is the memorable act of faith of the Republic, when the pious Godfrey of Bouillon, waging war to recover the sepulchre of the Son of Man from the hands of the unbelievers (for which endeavour many European princes and captains had allied themselves following the exhortations of Peter of Amiens the Hermit, who is seen in front of Doge Vitale Michiel), sent two hundred ships for that enterprise under the direction of Enrico Contarini Bishop of Castello and of Michele son of the doge, bringing the assistance of plentiful provisions to the Christian army. The galleys, prepared with gilded lanterns and flags waving in the wind, can be seen in the sea, ready to depart.

In the other one is depicted the act of justice done by Prince Antonio Venier upon the person of his own son, condemning him to be imprisoned for life; and in the distance he is carried off to the prisons.

He also has among the mythological subjects a Venus slightly smaller than life-size in the arms of a satyr, who looks at her and laughs;[167] and here with great intelligence the painter paired the deformity of

166. Pinacoteca Nazionale, Lucca 167. Galleria degli Uffizi, Contini Bonacossi Collection, Florence

the savage man with the beauty of that goddess; therefore she appears more beautiful, and he painted her with every delicacy. She also smiles seeing Love asleep upon the emerald of the grass and the gems of the flowers; while having escaped the gaze of watchful Cupid she freely entertains herself with the rustic Silenus. In which figure it is true that a painted beauty does not have less power to enslave hearts than a living one. And Europa sitting on the back of the insidious bull with many maidens around.[168]

There are also two inventions, of Paradise with a number of the Blessed over clouds placed on several circles, as Paolo was supposed to paint the picture for the Great Council together with Bassano, the part of the Trinity and the angels being allotted to him, as more fitting to his style; which did not happen because he was interrupted by death, when God called him to paint the blessed rooms of Heaven.[169]

The other one is of the naval battle against Selim, King of the Turks, where there are numerous ships with gilded sterns, weapons, standards and endless soldiers, with many of the enemies killed; in which,

168. Possibly Pinacoteca Capitolina, Rome
169. Musée des Beaux-Arts, Lille

*Opposite: Allegory of the Battle of Lepanto, ca. 1572*

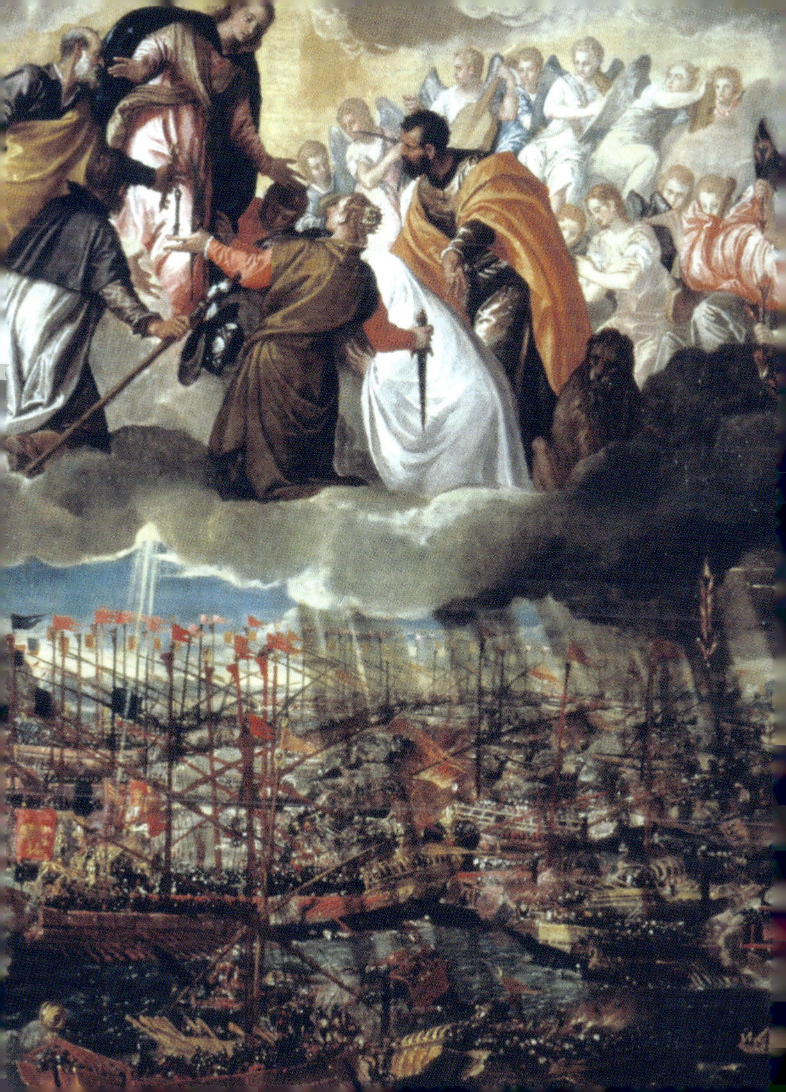

among those horrors, Paolo made death appear beautiful. At the top is the Virgin praying in front of the throne of the Trinity, and Venice kneeling between the imploring Saints Mark and Justina, through whose intercessions the Christian princes attained victory.[170] And there are two modelli of the painting of Pope Alexander III, but the works were differently painted by the sons, as we will discuss.

He also has the portrait of Pope Pius V, and that of Paolo painted by himself in the mirror, some dogs painted from nature, and other delightful things, and many drawings in chiaroscuro on coloured paper, that are not to be praised less than the painted works, since Paolo also drew with incomparable facility and felicity; which are kept with great care by the said Signor Caliari, together with the gold chain given by the Procurators of Saint Mark's to Paolo, as we said, for his works in the Library.

And finally let us talk about his studies, faithfully recounting what we heard from his disciples and from those who worked with him. Paolo, then, as we hinted in the beginning, was endowed by Heaven with an extraordinary disposition for that art, applying himself to study and labour as a youth. At the

170. Probably Accademia, Venice

beginning of his education he copied the works of Badile his master and the prints of Dürer, and he continued to use certain elements of their folds in the depiction of draperies, executing them however in an easier and quicker manner. As an adult, he enjoyed Parmigianino's drawings, copying many of them. He learnt from good reliefs (as excellent painters have always done) the strength of the contours, the firmness of muscles, the observation of shadows, the strong contrasts which are formed with the light of a lantern, which cannot be practised so straightforwardly from life; and his heir still owns many heads, arms and figures in gesso cast from the antique, which Paolo often used (as we have already said) in the works for the Council of Ten and in other places. Some though believed that as in his works he used many fancies and ornaments, he had in his house a heap of models dressed in various clothes and with hairstyles put together in various ways, which many painters usually collect; but because he was able to call upon a good memory, he depicted everything he saw using nothing more than his imagination; and was always able to add grace and nobility to his inventions.

His aim was also to imitate Nature, a target that every painter seeks; but unhappy is the one who does not know how to depart from pure imitation because of the defects of which she is full. But because Paolo was of a noble intellect and was not satisfied with ordinary appearances, he painted her more beautiful than she is. And it was useful above all for him to have practiced the Venetian manner, which has enlightened every painter, improving his methods of colouring after he came to Venice, since he knew that the style of Titian and Tintoretto was the most praised, as the one that was the closest to nature. And because it happened several times that he had to paint in competition with the same Tintoretto, he had the chance to exercise his intellect, as these two sublime minds tried to surpass each other through virtue: so that on many occasions they left the world divided in the judgment of their works. Hence if Tintoretto in many of his paintings displayed greater labour in art, in depicting his figures with erudite forms, lively attitudes and with a grandiose manner and energy in colouring, creating such witty conceits that could not be trumped, Veronese, on the other hand, for his magnificent inventions, for the beauty of his subjects, for the charm of his faces, for the variety of his physiognomies, for the attractiveness and for the infinite delights which he included in his works, to which he gave such an elegant symmetry which is usually called grace, is considered to have embellished Painting with every pomp and adornment. So that placed amongst such dubious and arbitrary rivalries, one has to conclude that one was Castor and the other Pollux in the heaven of Painting, and that in the guise of new Atlases they held such a noble weight, both benefiting with their paintings as examples, experimenting with various inventions and with the most accurate artifices of art.

We have to add to Paolo's honour that (as also with Tintoretto) there was no important public or private work by him, that was not copied by the students of drawing and colouring, to learn how to create the nobility and delight that invite all eyes to contemplation, because the beauty of objects is the spell that bewitches hearts.

His fame was also greatly increased by the prints made by Carracci after many of his inventions, such as the altarpiece of Santa Giustina in Padua; the one of the marriage of Saint Catherine in her church in Venice; the Purification of Our Lady from the organ of San Sebastiano, copied in folio by Villamena; the Crucifix in the same church. The altarpiece of Saint Anthony in San Francesco della Vigna, described above, was also engraved by Carracci; and the one of the resurrected Christ by Kilian; and two of the aforementioned Feasts, with other inventions transferred to copper by Flemish engravers, all continually promote his fame.

The paintings dispersed in the most famous galleries of Europe also bear witness to the taste for this celebrated painter universal amongst the most important princes and lords; such expense has been lavished in the collection of them that no palace does in fact appear properly adorned if it lacks a work by his hand. Tapestries and room-hangings of woven silk and gold are valued by people for the quality of the materials; excellent paintings to the contrary are esteemed by connoisseurs as part of the intellect; so it is that a clay vase sculpted by an illustrious hand should be admired more than a gold one made without craft or art. Thus that most learned poet, describing the carved doors in the palace of Armida, said:

> Le porte quì d'effigiato argento
> Sui cardini stridean di lucid'oro;
> Fermar ne le figure il guardo intento,
> Che vinta la materia è dal lavoro.*

* The door-leaves framed of carved silver-plate,/ Upon their golden hinges turn and twine./ They stayed to view this work of wit and state./ The workmanship excelled the substance fine. Tasso, *Gerusalemmme Liberata*, Canto XVI, translated by Edward Fairfax.

Now let us move to comment on the qualities of his heart, because often it happens that virtue can remain overshadowed by bad behaviour. Man is born in this world to dominate, as Ovid sang:

> Sanctus his animal mentisque capacious altæ
> Deerat adhuc et quod dominari in cætera posset.§

It is not given to every man to hold the sceptre, but virtue and moral character nonetheless afford us a way to advance in honour, as Paolo did, who became famous for his many praiseworthy actions. He had generous thoughts, which he displayed in his works, because every cause produces results which look like her. He was always very honest in his business; he never went out of his way to obtain any commission; nor did he degrade his position with low dealings; he always observed his promises and in every action he obtained praise. He wore precious clothes and velvet shoes, which are still kept by his heir. He ruled his family with great prudence, keeping his children away from harmful acquaintances and practices, teaching them with every piety about religious

§...the creature wanting was,/ Farre more devine, of nobler minde, which should the residue passe/In depth of knowledge, reason, wit, and high capacitie,/And which of all the residue should the Lord and ruler bee. Ovid, *Metamorphoses* I, translated by Arthur Golding.

observance and moral disciplines (a worthy painter should always be correct and cautious). He lived away from luxury; and he was careful in expenditure, so that he was able to buy many farms and accumulate wealth and furnishings worthy of any knight, leaving his sons well settled with property so that they were able to live suitably without hardship or effort.

He attained the grace and favour of the great, the love of the masters, the respect of all those who knew him, and Aliense the painter told me that having met Titian in Saint Mark's Square, Paolo greeted him with due reverence, and was affectionately hugged by Titian who added that it made him happy to consider Paolo as uniting in his person the decorum and the nobility of Painting.

Invited to serve Philip II, King of Spain, to decorate some of the rooms at the Escorial, he refused to go, because he was busy with his works in the Doge's Palace and encumbered by many affairs, and sorry to leave his own nest for adventure, because it has rightly been said, *Domus optima,** as everybody is most keen to live in his own house; and Federico Zuccari from Sant'Angelo in Vado went in his place. Zuccari, when he was in Venice, often visited his friend Paolo,

* Home is best

and acquired a few mementos from his hands, and I heard the old painters often say that Zuccari copied the two paintings of the chapel of San Sebastiano in drawings; and in one of his poems he makes Painting describe the gifts she has received from painters, mentioning Paolo thus:

> But what will I say of Paolo Veronese,
> Magnanimous, courteous, and excellent,
> Who brought to a conclusion a thousand
> beautiful ventures.
>
> Of the most beautiful gems of the Orient
> He placed a necklace around my neck,
> And of candid pearls a large pendant.

A number of memorable sayings are attributed to Paolo; that good judgment of Painting could only be achieved by those who were well instructed in the art, and that ability was a gift of Heaven; and that labouring at that without natural talent was like sowing in the waves; that the most praiseworthy part of a painter was simplicity and modesty; and that the images of saints and angels should be painted by excellent painters, since they must incite admiration and sympathy. He revered Titian as the father of art, and he esteemed very much Tintoretto's lively mind, being only sorry that he brought disrepute upon the masters by painting in every manner, which led precisely to the destruction of the essence of the profession and its livelihood.

Archytas was able to make wooden doves and with art give them flight; there was he [Albertus Magnus] who gave speech to a skull; he [Dædalus] who dared to stroll along the paths of the air, and he [Berthold Shwarz]who locked up Jupiter's lightning in perforated bronzes, only to unleash them at his own will with prodigious marvel; but Paolo in the end did things that were even greater. He favoured joy, celebrated beauty, rendered laughter more cheerful and he inspired the senses of life in the images that he painted.

Finally, we now arrive at the funeral obsequies of our divine painter. The Graces, Venuses and Loves, whose beauties were so decorously painted by his brush and their honours depicted, shall dress in lugubrious mourning garments as a sign of grief; and Painting clad in a black cloak shall inconsolably sigh her loss now that Paolo dies. The Nymphs will bring myrtles and cypresses to decorate his coffin; the Muses will groan lugubriously and will sing dirges with sad elegies. With reason we weep at every mortal end, as a precious creation of the hands of God is undone, of which Ovid sang:

Natus homo est, sive hunc divino semine fecit
Ille Opifex rerum Mundi melioris origo.*

But more tears shall be shed for Paolo's death, since that loss seems greater when it is of something that is more praiseworthy.

It was the year 1588 when God decided to take Paolo from the world still in the prime of his life, to demonstrate that such gifts are only given to mortals for a short time; he was taking part in a solemn procession for the indulgence granted by Christ's Vicar Sixtus V, and, heated by the journey, he was attacked by a violent fever, and died aged 58 on the second feast of Easter, fortunate also in flying to Heaven laden with divine grace at the moment of his death.

The world sighed at such heavy loss and Heaven rejoiced as it welcomed such a pure soul. The body was then buried with a funeral ceremony by his brother and sons in San Sebastiano, in the midst of his work, as that theatre of glory, which he had created with his brush, was his only worthy sepulchre; and next to the organ they placed his effigy majestically sculpted by Camillo Bozzetti; which after some time his last son Gabriele had renovated by Matteo Carneri with this inscription:

* Man was created! Did the Unknown God designing then a better world make man of seed divine? Ovid, *Metamorphoses*, trans. More.

PAULO CALIARIO VERONENSI

PICTORI NATURÆ ÆMULO,

ARTIS MIRACULO,

SUPERSTITE FATIS

FAMA VICTURO*

And over the stone slab which covers his bones they placed this brief memorial:

PAULO CALIARIO VERON.

PICTORI CELEBERRIMO

FILIJ & BENEDIC. FRATER PIENTISS.

& SIBI POSTERISQUE.

DECESSIT XII KALEND. MAIJ

MDLXXXVIII*

It was not possible on that narrow slab to enclose all those immortal merits, worthy of being recorded by the hand of eternity amongst the resplendent

* To Paolo Caliari Veronese, painter, emulator of nature, miracle of art, assured of victory over the fates by surviving fame

* To Paul Caliari Veronese, painter most famous, his sons and Benedetto his brother most devoted both to him and to his descendants. Died XII Kalends of May [19 April] 1588

images of Andromeda, Cassiopeia and Perseus in the Heavens.

*By the Most Excellent Signor Nicolò Crasso:*

While with learned hand you paint and colour
Celestial forms over a caduceus canvas,
Which new Idea did you have in your great mind,
Paolo, in whom every other merit contracts in one?

You simulate the counterfeit more alive than life,
And you graft the soul and senses in the colours,
You waken ardent loves in cold bosoms,
When you decorate and paint beauty on canvases.

His soul takes flight in amazement,
To see the soul your colours give the painted papers,
So that one loses his movement and the other takes them.

What more? If she makes a perfect thing in part,
Always she asks for advice from your works,
And you are the example for both Nature and Art.

*By Signor Pietro Michiel Venetian Nobleman:*

Of the singing intelligence,
Of a Catullus he boasts,
Between his banks the sonorous Adige.
But then while he admires

With what strength and how much
It has in conquering Nature
The Painting of Paolo,
The marvels of the canvas he admires,
And says in his own language, surrender the laurel
Surrender, now that the one has been beaten by the other
The pen by the brush.

*Naturæ & Artis Pauli Caliari Veronensis Pictoris celeberrimi duellum.*

O' pulchrum vasta mundi certamen arena,
Hinc Natura atque hinc Ars, Caliare, tua.
Mortales tanto præsunt, Divique duello,
Vt laudis victrix prœmia digna ferat.
At longe imparibus mire concurritur armis;
Marte tamen contra statur utrinque pari.
Illa calore potens, hæc vano freta colore,
Hæc fictis, veris impetit illa viris.
Hæc umbris claræ contendit strenua luci
Illius & falsis fallit imaginibus.
Nativo pictum, solidoque opponit inane,
Ludit & innumeris ingeniosa modis.
Effusa aspiceres vento volitantia signa,
Et galeis cristas surgere terrificas;
Loricas clypeosque ex ære, auroque rigentes,
Fulmineos enses, flammiferasque faces,

Et pictas pharetras, arcus, volucresque sagittas,
Ingentes hastas, iactaque pila manu;
Intrepidas equitum turmas prorumpere in hostes,
Turbare & cuneos, signa canente tuba.
Nec pugne finis. Virtuti cedere virtus
Nescia, conflictu fertur in arma novo.
Quæ tandem ancipiti detur sententia lance?
Ambæ victrices, utraque victa fuit.*

*M. Antonij Romiti I.C.*

*O, what a magnificent contest, setting Nature against your Art, Caliari. Mortals as well as gods [must] preside over such a duel, in order that the victor may obtain the reward of commensurate praise. But the amazing struggle is fought with heavily unequal arms, though martial vigour is the same on either side. The one full of living warmth, the other supplied with insubstantial colours. Aligning fictive forces to match real ones, strenuously advancing shadows against light, and deceiving with false images, opposing the painted to the original, and to the solid the hollow, it plays ingeniously in many modes. You will see unfurled standards offered to the wind, and terrifying crests erect on helmets; corslets and shields made hard by bronze and gold, thundering swords and flame-throwing torches, and painted quivers, bows and flying arrows, immense spears and javelins thrown by hand; intrepid squadrons of horse rushing towards the enemy and breaking up serried formations to the sound of signalling trumpets. Nor is there an end to the fight. Valour not knowing how to cede to valour, battle is joined anew. What evenly poised balance could give the verdict? Both were victors and both succumbed in equal measure.

## LIST OF ILLUSTRATIONS

All work oil on canvas, unless otherwise stated.

This edition published 2014 by
Pallas Athene (Publishers) Ltd,
Studio 11B, Archway Studios, 25-27 Bickerton Road, London N19 5JT
**www.pallasathene.co.uk**
© Pallas Athene 2014
Printed in England

ISBN 978 1 84368 097 0

All texts translated for this edition by Xavier F. Salomon,
except for the inscriptions on pp. 168, 105, 145, 147, 186
and the poem on pp. 188-9 which are by Christopher Ligota

Half title: Detail from ceiling decoration of the Sala dell'Olimpo,
Villa Barbaro at Maser, ca. 1560
Frontispiece and jacket: Young huntsman (possibly a self-portrait),
Villa Barbaro at Maser, ca. 1560

All illustrations courtesy of museums and other owners,
except on pp. 13, 15, 32, 71, 83, 89, 90, 100
which are courtesy Dr. Emil Krén,
Web Gallery of Art, http://www.wga.hu.
and the cover photograph, which is courtesy Xavier F. Salomon
Special thanks to Lisa Adams

ACKNOWLEDGEMENTS

Susan Ghosh, Sarah Moulden, Valentina Ravaglia, and Emanuela Tarizzo
have provided immense help with the translations of Veronese's *Lives*.
Thanks also to Christopher Ligota for his translations,
and to Nicholas Cullinan, Jennifer Fletcher,
Helen Langdon, Nicholas Penny and Kevin Petkos.
This book is dedicated to Fiora Gandolfi Herrera,
without whom Venice would be less 'Serenissima'.